DATE DUE

DEC 2 0 2011

12/10/14

ISSUES THAT CONCERN YOU

Drunk Driving

Christine Van Tuyl, *Book Editor*

Bonnie Szumski, *Publisher*
Helen Cothran, *Managing Editor*

GREENHAVEN PRESS

An imprint of Thomson Gale, a part of The Thomson Corporation

THOMSON

GALE

Detroit • New York • San Francisco • San Diego • New Haven, Conn. • Waterville, Maine • London • Munich

THOMSON

★ ™

GALE

© 2006 Thomson Gale, a part of The Thomson Corporation.

Thomson and Star Logo are trademarks and Gale and Greenhaven Press are registered trademarks used herein under license.

For more information, contact
Greenhaven Press
27500 Drake Rd.
Farmington Hills, MI 48331-3535
Or you can visit our Internet site at http://www.gale.com

LIBRARY OF CONGRESS CATALOGING-IN-PUBLICATION DATA

Drunk driving / Christine Van Tuyl, book editor.
  p. cm. — (Issues That Concern You)
    Includes bibliographical references and index.
  ISBN 0-7377-3239-3 (lib. : alk. paper)
  1. Drunk driving—United States. 2. Drunk driving—United States—Prevention. I. Van Tuyl, Christine. II. Series
  HE5620.D72D78 2006
  363.12'57—dc22

                                              2005055077

Printed in the United States of America

CONTENTS

Just a few years ago, Jacqui Saburido was a beautiful, twenty-year-old from Caracas, Venezuela, studying English as an exchange student in Austin, Texas. She loved to dance flamenco, listen to music, and hang out with her friends. Today Jacqui is unrecognizable. Third-degree burns cover her entire face and most of her body. She has no lips, no nose, no hair, and only part of one ear. A flap of skin hides her left eye, and her fingers are amputated.

On the evening of September 19, 1999, Jacqui was with friends as they drove home from a birthday party on a dark road on the outskirts of Austin. Nearby, eighteen-year-old Reggie Stephey had been drinking beer with his buddies. He decided to drive home anyway. At some point along the road home, Reggie drove his GMC Yukon across the yellow center lines, smashing into the car carrying Jacqui and her four friends. The car quickly caught on fire and burned. Two of the passengers in Jacqui's car died, and two of them survived with injuries. Jacqui suffered severe burns. Almost three hours after the fiery crash, Reggie had a blood alcohol concentration (BAC) level of .13, well over the legal limit of .08. He was sentenced to seven years in prison, eligible for parole in four.

Jacqui is just one of an estimated half a million people injured in alcohol-related crashes every year. Thousands more are killed in such accidents. While the total number of alcohol-related driving fatalities has decreased slightly in recent years, from 17,524 in 2002 to 16,694 in 2004, it remains alarmingly high. Thirty-nine percent of traffic deaths occur in drunk driving accidents, an average of one death every thirty minutes. In addition to deaths and injuries, drunk driving exacts a crippling economic price. Alcohol-related crashes cost the American public an estimated $114.3 billion each year.

Despite the human and economic toll, people continue to drink and drive, and in increasing numbers. According to a survey published in the May 2005 issue of the *American Journal of Preventive Medicine*, Americans reported driving under the influence of alcohol 159 million times in 2002 (compared to 116 million in 1997).

In another survey conducted in 2005 by Gallup on behalf of Mothers Against Drunk Driving (MADD), 60 percent of those surveyed (1,004 people) said they had operated a car or truck under the influence of alcohol, up from 57 percent in 2000.

Young people are not immune to the effects of drunk driving. In 2004, 5,896 people between the ages of sixteen and twenty were killed in automobile accidents in the United States. Of these, 2,115 (36 percent) were killed in alcohol-related crashes. In addition, of all drivers between the age of sixteen and twenty who were involved in alcohol-related crashes, 17 percent had blood-alcohol concentrations greater than .08. Thus, despite laws that

According to the National Highway Traffic Safety Administration, approximately 17,000 alcohol-related traffic fatalities occur each year.

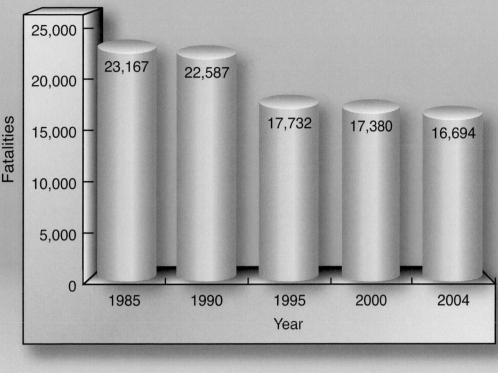

U.S. Alcohol-Related Traffic Fatalities

Source: National Highway Traffic Safety Administration, January 2006.

forbid drinking under the age of twenty-one, young people con-tinue to drink and suffer the consequences behind the wheel.

Legislators have passed numerous laws in an effort to prevent drunk driving among America's youth. In fact, the national legal drinking age was set at twenty-one with this goal specifically in mind. In the 1970s, states were allowed to set their own drinking age, and many states allowed those eighteen and older to drink. In 1984, Congress required all states to raise the age to twenty-one or else forfeit much-needed federal highway repair dollars. All states subsequently complied with the new mandate.

Supporters of the age-twenty-one law insist it has been a great success. While conceding that it has not entirely eliminated drink-ing among those under twenty-one, advocates insist that the new

Experts debate whether setting the minimum legal drinking age at twenty-one has led to fewer drunk driving tragedies.

law has greatly reduced drunk driving deaths in America. The Centers for Disease Control and Prevention reports that the number of crashes involving drivers sixteen to seventeen who have been drinking has decreased by 60 percent since the law went into effect. The National Highway Traffic Safety Administration estimates that over 20,000 lives have been saved by the law's passage.

As journalist Stephen Chapman states, "Drinking and driving used to be the leading cause of death among teenagers. Not anymore."

Critics dispute the effectiveness of the age-twenty-one law. For example, David J. Hanson, a professor of sociology at the State University of New York, cites studies that show no difference in alcohol consumption before and after the imposition of the higher drinking age. Hanson and others insist that prohibiting alcohol consumption among young people is not the solution to alcohol-related problems such as drunk driving. In their view, forbidding drinking simply increases its appeal for young people and forces them to drink sneakily and irresponsibly. Rather, teens must be introduced to alcohol at a young age and taught how do drink in moderation. "People become responsible by being properly taught, given responsibility, and then held accountable for their actions," Hanson concludes.

The minimum drinking age is just one of many strategies designed to address the problem of drunk driving. Authors in this anthology examine drinking-age laws and other controversial issues related to this topic, including BAC laws, sobriety checkpoints, and forced blood draws. In addition, the volume contains several appendixes to help the reader understand and explore the topic, including a thorough bibliography and a list of organizations to contact for further information. The appendix entitled "What You Should Know About Drunk Driving" offers crucial facts about drunk driving and its impact on young people. The appendix "What You Should Do About Drunk Driving" offers tips to young people who may confront the problem of drunk driving in their own lives. With all these features, *Issues That Concern You: Drunk Driving* provides an excellent resource for everyone interested in this pressing issue.

ONE

DUI Laws Should Be More Strictly Enforced

Mothers Against Drunk Driving

> In the following report Mothers Against Drunk Driving (MADD) argues that too many Americans are dying of alcohol-related traffic crashes—an average of one person every half hour. Law enforcement agencies desperately need to fight drunk driving by enforcing DUI (driving under the influence) laws. Unfortunately, MADD contends, many law enforcement agencies are inadequately funded, and their officers lack the proper training to effectively stop drunk drivers. The war against drunk drivers must be a top priority. Funding must be increased, officers must undergo better training, and the entire system for stopping drunk drivers must be drastically improved. Better enforcement is the only way to reduce alcohol-related traffic deaths and injuries, MADD concludes. Mothers Against Drunk Driving is a nonprofit organization with more than six hundred chapters nationwide. MADD's mission is to stop drunk driving, support the victims of this crime, and prevent underage drinking.

In the last several years, America has witnessed a disturbing trend. After nearly two decades of decreasing alcohol-related traffic fatalities, the course changed. Alcohol-related traffic fatalities have flat-lined.

Until recently, America made great progress—shedding the mentality that drunk driving was a socially acceptable "accident" and adopting the correct view that drunk driving is a serious, preventable crime. Still, unacceptable numbers of parents are burying their children. Too many kids are mourning their parents. And every citizen, politician, judge and law enforcement officer in the country should take notice.

Women who have lost loved ones to drunk drivers participate in a candlelight vigil held by Mothers Against Drunk Driving in Nashville, Tennessee.

Unfortunately, those in the last group often feel a squeeze. Stretched thin in today's post-9/11 world, law enforcement agencies often lack resources to implement proven DUI countermeasures, such as highly visible, publicized DUI checkpoints. Meanwhile, officers often lack sufficient training and are evaluated on how many DUI arrests they've made, not by how many alcohol-related crashes they have prevented.

Glynn Birch, national president of Mothers Against Drunk Driving, stands by a promotional poster aimed at discouraging teens from drinking.

It is time for change. That is why more than 50 law enforcement executives and other traffic safety leaders gathered at the first-ever MADD Law Enforcement Leadership Summit in January 2004. MADD listened as those with experience—stopping drunk drivers, administering sobriety tests, and knocking on the doors of victims' families—discussed the problems and brainstormed solutions. Together, Summit participants reviewed scientific studies that showed what works.

Their feedback was critical to help MADD develop solid, science-based recommendations that will result in a trend everyone can support: fewer alcohol-related traffic deaths and injuries.

MADD Recommendations

- Advocate general deterrence approaches that prevent death and injury
- Re-prioritization of prevention by law enforcement leadership
- Promote paid advertising to ensure highly publicized enforcement efforts
- Increase resources for effective enforcement
- Emphasize the need to train officers
- Enhance system efficiency and effectiveness

The Situation

While alcohol-related traffic fatalities generally decreased in the 1980s and early 1990s—flat lining in the late 1990s, no significant progress has been made in recent years. In 2003, 17,013 Americans died in alcohol-related traffic crashes—an average of one person every half hour. Another 500,000 people were injured in traffic crashes where alcohol was involved.

Each person killed or injured has loved ones who now share the same voice. Together, we're MADD, and we are working tirelessly to bring the death and heartache on our highways to a stop.

This will require careful steps—steps rooted in proven methods rather than hopes or best intentions. What follows are condensed versions of the science-based methods reviewed by Law Enforcement Summit participants—science that sets the stage for recommendations issued in . . . this report.

The Science

Centers for Disease Control (CDC) study shows sobriety checkpoints reduce alcohol-related crashes
Fewer alcohol-related crashes occur when sobriety checkpoints are implemented, according to a report published in the December 2002 issue of *Traffic Injury Prevention*.

Led by CDC scientists, a team of experts conducted a systematic review of 23 scientifically sound studies from around the world and concluded that sobriety checkpoints consistently and effectively reduce alcohol-related crashes and the fatalities and injuries related to these crashes.

In fact, the research showed that where selective breath testing checkpoints—those that require police to have reason to suspect the driver has been drinking before administering a breath test—were used, there was a median decrease of 20 percent for fatal and nonfatal alcohol-related crashes.

An added benefit: checkpoints often also result in the arrest of drivers for other offenses such as driving with a suspended license or carrying weapons.

Second CDC study ties DUI countermeasures to less drunk driving
A second study by the CDC suggests that strong state legislative, enforcement and education activities to prevent drunk driving reduces the rate of drinking and driving. The study, published in the June 2002 issue of *Injury Prevention*, demonstrates that residents of states with weaker DUI legislation, enforcement and education activities were more likely to drive while impaired.

The study used MADD's Rating the States 2000 survey as an index of each state's comprehensive DUI prevention activities and examined these against individuals' self-reported drinking and driving behavior.

A MADD banner hanging on a Miami street encourages designated drivers to completely abstain from alcohol in order to prevent drunk driving.

People living in states that received a MADD grade of "D" were 60 percent more likely to report alcohol impaired driving than those living in "A" states.

Checkpoint Tennessee: Highly Publicized Efforts Reduce Fatal Crashes

A statewide sobriety checkpoint program conducted in 1994–1995 also demonstrates that publicity and visibility reduce drunk driving in the short and long term.

The program, called Checkpoint Tennessee, was funded by the National Highway Traffic Safety Administration (NHTSA) to determine if highly publicized checkpoints conducted throughout the state on a weekly basis would have an effect on impaired driving. The study showed a 20 percent reduction in alcohol-related fatal crashes extending at least 21 months after the program ended. Meanwhile, five comparison states showed a statistically insignificant increase in alcohol-related fatal crashes coincident with Checkpoint Tennessee.

The CDC studies and Checkpoint Tennessee combine with other studies to demonstrate the overwhelming reality: highly publicized, frequent and visible enforcement efforts, especially sobriety checkpoints, will reduce alcohol-related deaths.

The Summit

The recommendations set forth by MADD in this report were developed with input from more than 50 partners. Participants in the 2004 Law Enforcement Summit included executive level representatives of law enforcement agencies across the country, as well as critical players from the nation's leading law enforcement professional associations.

Participants also included staff or representatives from state and federal government agencies, traffic safety groups, and MADD.

Summit participants reviewed research-based deterrence strategies and reported on successful initiatives in their jurisdictions. They discussed enforcement barriers, motivation, resource challenges, and the complexity of the arrest process.

Consensus was not a goal of the meeting, yet it emerged in a single sentence: frequent, high-visibility enforcement is critical to preventing impaired driving. This chief recommendation—bolstered by five additional recommendations—will result in an outcome everyone in the law enforcement community can support: fewer alcohol-related traffic deaths and injuries.

A police officer cites a driver for a traffic violation while other officers search for impaired drivers at a sobriety checkpoint in Miami.

Recommendation #1: Advocate General Deterrence Approaches That Prevent Death and Injury

General deterrence, the concept of preventing a crime before it occurs, is the most important strategy we can employ to reduce the growing number of fatal alcohol-related crashes. Impaired driving and seat belt enforcement mobilizations exemplify general deterrence by concentrating and coordinating law enforcement efforts during a specific period of time. Conducted nationally or statewide, mobilizations use paid and earned media to alert the public to stepped-up enforcement efforts. The primary goal is not to "bust" DUI offenders. The goal is to deter drunk driving. As one Summit participant put it: "Checkpoints are about police presence, not the number of DUIs issued."

Enforcement blitzes, while highly effective, cannot replace daily enforcement and education. We must make every effort—in every state—to use high-visibility enforcement as a routine strategy to deter individuals from driving impaired.

Sobriety checkpoints

Sobriety checkpoints are the most effective general deterrence enforcement tactic available to law enforcement officers today. In fact, research shows that checkpoints can reduce alcohol-related crashes and fatalities by 18 to 24 percent. Checkpoints work because they increase the perception among drivers that arrest is likely if they drink and drive. The result is fewer alcohol-related crashes, deaths and injuries.

However, law enforcement agencies currently lack adequate funding to implement and maintain checkpoint programs on a regular basis. In turn, law enforcement agencies must use their resources efficiently—research shows that as few as three officers can conduct a checkpoint without any loss of effectiveness.

Other high-visibility enforcement strategies

MADD recognizes that sobriety checkpoints are not possible or appropriate for all communities. In such areas, well-publicized and highly visible saturation patrol or wolf pack efforts are powerful substitutes. Saturation patrols and checkpoint efforts often use multiple law enforcement agencies to concentrate their resources

Roses and informative literature sit on the chairs of MADD members who will participate in a memorial ceremony in Coral Gables, Florida.

on a particular geographic area to identify and arrest impaired motorists.

Next steps

- Encourage law enforcement agencies to use general deterrence strategies, especially sobriety checkpoints, where possible
- Use saturation patrols or wolf pack efforts if checkpoints are not possible
- Urge policy and decision makers to allocate sufficient resources to fund high-visibility enforcement efforts

Recommendation #2: Re-Prioritization of Prevention by Law Enforcement Leadership

Law enforcement leaders must make the prevention of alcohol-related crashes a priority—both within their communities and within their departments.

First, law enforcement leaders should advocate the need to conduct frequent, high-visibility enforcement efforts, especially sobriety checkpoints. While scientific studies demonstrate that such enforcement efforts will reduce alcohol-related crashes, such findings are worthless if law enforcement leaders fail to implement these proven enforcement efforts in their communities.

Secondly, law enforcement leaders should examine the criteria by which they measure departmental success. MADD urges law enforcement leaders to base their success on the reduction in DUI crashes, injuries and fatalities—not just the number of DUI arrests.

An intoxicated driver tries to walk a straight line as he undergoes a sobriety test under the watchful eyes of two police officers.

The nature of performance evaluations is that administrators understandably try to build in measurable outcomes. DUI arrests are easily measurable. However, a higher number of DUI arrests will not necessarily reduce the number of alcohol-related fatalities.

As one Summit participant put it: "We do evaluate our troops' performance on the numbers . . . but we need to evaluate them on the outcomes of their work. Otherwise, we send a conflicting message."

The bottom line: law enforcement leaders are critical to making a difference in the fight against impaired drivers. By creating a sense of priority and urgency about this grave safety threat, law enforcement leaders can set the tone and motivate officers on the front lines to make our roads safer for everyone.

Next steps
- Urge law enforcement leaders to make frequent, high-visibility enforcement efforts a higher priority
- Encourage law enforcement leaders to redefine successful impaired driving enforcement—counting reductions in alcohol-related crashes, injuries and fatalities instead of just DUI arrests

Recommendation #3: Promote Paid Advertising to Ensure Highly Publicized Enforcement Efforts

Paid advertising is one of the reasons sobriety checkpoints and other enforcement strategies work. Effective paid advertising reliably increases the perception among drivers that arrest is likely if they drink and drive.

Case in point: In May 2002, the ten states that conducted Click It or Ticket (zero tolerance safety belt law enforcement) efforts with paid advertising saw safety belt use increase from 68.5 to 77.1 percent over a four-week period. States that relied only on earned media to publicize their increased enforcement efforts achieved a meager average gain of half a percentage point.

MADD strongly encourages the continued use of federal funding for paid national media campaigns to augment current earned media efforts that accompany intensive impaired driving and seat belt enforcement efforts.

Currently, NHTSA provides grants to states to fund many local law enforcement agencies' mobilizations and saturation efforts at certain times throughout the year. These efforts have a cumulative effect, and are even more successful when they integrate paid advertising that reinforces a strong enforcement message.

Next steps

- Advocate the continued use of federal funding to support paid national media campaigns that accompany intensive impaired driving and seat belt enforcement efforts
- Urge federal, state and local leaders to allocate funds to support integrated enforcement and media efforts on a day to day basis to remind people that reducing alcohol-related traffic death and injury is an everyday concern

Recommendation #4: Increase Resources for Effective Enforcement

The challenges before public safety departments today are varied and great. However, even in today's post-9/11 world, traffic enforcement in general, and impaired driving enforcement in particular, must be higher on the list of law enforcement's priorities. To successfully achieve that goal, agencies need continued resources allocated to this critical task.

With law enforcement budgets stretched to their limits, funding assistance is critical for DUI training, overtime, and equipment to ensure effective enforcement.

At the same time, states and NHTSA must be accountable for the expenditure of federal highway safety funds, and states must work cooperatively with NHTSA to develop strategic highway safety plans that establish goals and evaluation measures for funded programs.

Next steps

- Local, state and federal policy makers must provide increased and continued funding for effective impaired driving and seat belt enforcement
- Resources must fund efforts proven to reduce fatalities and injuries

Recommendation #5: Emphasize the Need to Train Officers

Even with demanding job responsibilities and tight budgets, time and money must be devoted to the training of officers in evidence gathering, arrest procedures and other areas related to enforcement of impaired driving laws.

First, officers must receive more training. The average law enforcement officer receives eight hours of training on impaired driving. This is insufficient. NHTSA and the National Criminal Justice Association (NCJA) recommend at least 40 hours of academy training on impaired driving. Additionally, officers should be required to update or refresh their skills each year.

A car with a smashed front end sits next to an anti–drunk driving sign, adding poignant emphasis to the sign's message.

Secondly, training must be consistent—Standardized Field Sobriety Testing (SFST) training should meet NHTSA/IACP [International Association of Chiefs of Police] standards. Consistent training leads to consistent application of the law.

Third, the content of training must be expanded. A Traffic Injury Research Foundation study found that about half of all law enforcement officers said they would take more enforcement action if they had more comprehensive training. Traffic safety groups agree that expanded training should come in areas such as: DUI prevention strategies, in-depth SFST, training, evidence gathering, arrest procedures and individual states' laws and statutes.

Next steps
- Increase the amount of training officers receive on impaired driving enforcement
- Adopt an approved training format
- Improve training content

Hitch. © 2005 by King Features Syndicate. Reproduced by permission.

Recommendation #6: Enhance System Efficiency and Effectiveness

Another important consensus that emerged from the Law Enforcement Leadership Summit: participants believe that if we are to successfully reduce the number of alcohol-related fatalities, we must enhance system efficiency and effectiveness. "Putting a drunk in jail has just gotten too complicated," one participant said succinctly.

Officers who execute a simple DUI arrest are often off the road for hours, processing paperwork instead of identifying other drunk drivers. Some departments across the country have instituted electronic reporting forms that streamline the arrest process and get officers back on the streets more quickly. In other states, legislatures have re-codified DUI laws to make them easier to understand and enforce. Efforts like this increase a department's efficiency, and allow officers to spend more time on actual enforcement.

MADD is committed to supporting these and other efforts within the system to reduce impaired driving. As Summit participants noted, once law enforcement has done its job, the legal system and the public must do theirs. For example:

- Public outcry must take place when judges have low DUI conviction rates
- Seasoned prosecutors must be retained, so police spend less time retraining officers of the court
- DUI offenders must be moved into assessment and treatment immediately, once they are in jail
- Tracking systems must be developed that review DUIs at every stage of the arrest and sanctioning process to determine where there might be issues

Support for Law Enforcement

Keeping America's roads safe is a daunting, necessary task. Our everyday heroes—law enforcement officers—are charged with the job. They deserve nothing less than our full support in gaining tools to do the job we ask them to do.

That is why MADD called experts together for the first-ever MADD Law Enforcement Leadership Summit. And that is why MADD commits to stepping up its support for law enforcement—working at every level to focus attention and secure resources for critically-needed enforcement.

The MADD recommendations outlined in this report are six steps in the right direction. The recommendations, if implemented, will equip most law enforcement departments with the means to conduct highly-publicized enforcement efforts, including sobriety checkpoints—the most effective tool available to them today. The recommendations will result in better funded, better motivated, better trained, more efficient law enforcement personnel.

And, in the end, the recommendations will help reduce the unacceptable number of alcohol-related traffic deaths and injuries. They will make America's roadways safer for everyone, every day.

Drunk Driving Laws Are Too Harsh

Radley Balko

In the following article, Radley Balko argues that courts and legislatures are steadily chipping away at the civil rights of people who are accused of driving under the influence of alcohol. For example, in 1990 the U.S. Supreme Court ruled in favor of roadblock sobriety checkpoints even though they violate citizens' Fourth Amendment right to protection against unreasonable search, according to Balko. In addition, the author contends, many state courts are instituting harsh legislation, including the right to revoke the driver's licenses of drunk driving defendants before they even go to trial. Moreover, in the majority of states, the penalties for drivers who refuse to take roadside sobriety tests are more severe than the penalties for drivers who take these tests and fail. In short, Balko concludes, DUI defendants no longer have the fundamental right to the presumption of innocence. Society needs to reevaluate its drunk driving laws and restore the criminal protections and civil liberties of motorists, Balko maintains. Radley Balko is a policy analyst for the Cato Institute, a libertarian public policy research foundation headquartered in Washington, D.C. Balko is also a columnist for FoxNews.com and has been published in *Time* magazine, the *Washington Post*, the *Los Angeles Times*, the *Chicago Sun Times*, Canada's *National Post*, and several other publications.

When Pennsylvanian Keith Emerich went to the hospital recently for an irregular heartbeat, he told his doctor he was a heavy drinker: a six-pack per day. Later, Pennsylvania's Department of Transportation sent Emerich a letter. His driver's license had been revoked. If Emerich wanted it back, he'd need to prove to Pennsylvania authorities that he was competent to drive. His doctor had turned him in, as required by state law.

The Pennsylvania law is old (it dates back to the 1960s), but it's hardly unusual. Courts and lawmakers have stripped DWI [drinking while intoxicated] defendants of the presumption of innocence—along with several other common criminal justice protections we afford to the likes of accused rapists, murderers and pedophiles.

In the 1990 case *Michigan v. Sitz,* the U.S. Supreme Court ruled that the magnitude of the drunken driving problem outweighed the "slight" intrusion into motorists' protections against unreasonable search effected by roadblock sobriety checkpoints. Writing for the majority, Chief Justice Rehnquist ruled that the 25,000 roadway deaths due to alcohol were reason enough to set aside the Fourth Amendment.

Exaggerated Statistics

The problem is that the 25,000 number was awfully misleading. It included any highway fatality in which alcohol was in any way involved: a sober motorist striking an intoxicated pedestrian, for example.

It's a number that's still used today. In 2002, the *Los Angeles Times* examined accident data and estimated that in the previous year, of the 18,000 "alcohol-related" traffic fatalities drunk driving activists cited the year before, only about 5,000 involved a drunk driver taking the life of a sober driver, pedestrian, or passenger.

Unfortunately, courts and legislatures still regularly cite the inflated "alcohol-related" number when justifying new laws that chip away at our civil liberties.

For example, the Supreme Court has ruled that states may legislate away a motorist's Sixth Amendment right to a jury trial and his Fifth Amendment right against self-incrimination. In 2002, the Supreme Court of Wisconsin ruled that police officers could forcibly extract blood from anyone suspected of drunk driving. Other courts have ruled that prosecutors aren't obligated to provide defendants with blood or breath test samples for independent testing (even though both are feasible and relatively cheap to do). In almost every other facet of criminal law, defendants are given access to the evidence against them.

Some states require doctors to report the blood alcohol concentration of patients involved in automobile accidents.

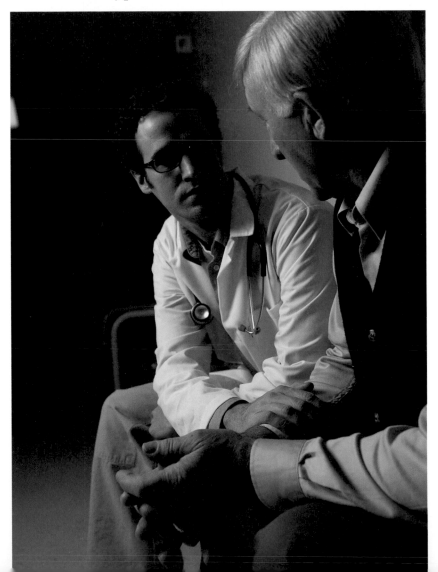

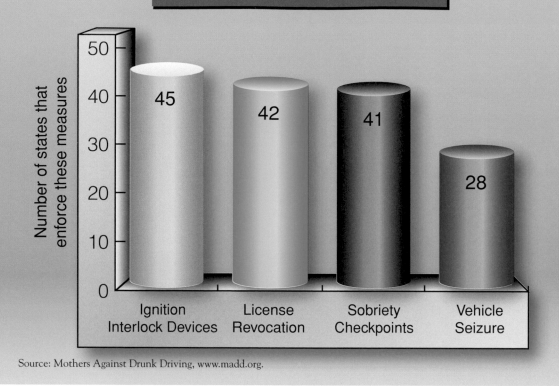

Anti–Drunk Driving Measure

Number of states that enforce these measures

Measure	Value
Ignition Interlock Devices	45
License Revocation	42
Sobriety Checkpoints	41
Vehicle Seizure	28

Source: Mothers Against Drunk Driving, www.madd.org.

Increasingly Harsh Penalties

These decisions haven't gone unnoticed in state legislatures. Forty-one states now reserve the right to revoke drunken driving defendants' licenses before they're ever brought to trial. Thirty-seven states now impose *harsher* penalties on motorists who refuse to take roadside sobriety tests than on those who take them and fail. Seventeen states have laws denying drunk driving defendants the same opportunities to plea bargain given to those accused of violent crimes.

Until recently, New York City cops could seize the cars of first-offender drunk driving suspects upon arrest. Those acquitted or otherwise cleared of charges were still required to file civil suits to get their cars back, which typically cost thousands of dollars. The city of Los Angeles still seizes the cars of suspected first-time drunk drivers, as well as the cars of those suspected of drug activity and soliciting prostitutes.

Newer laws are even worse. As of last month [June 2004], Washington State now requires anyone arrested (not convicted—*arrested*) for drunken driving to install an "ignition interlock" device, which forces the driver to blow into a breath test tube before starting the car, and at regular intervals while driving. A

A man blows into an ignition interlock device. The device is connected to an engine's ignition system and will prevent the vehicle from starting if it detects a blood alcohol concentration that is over a pre-set limit.

Interlock Safety Devices

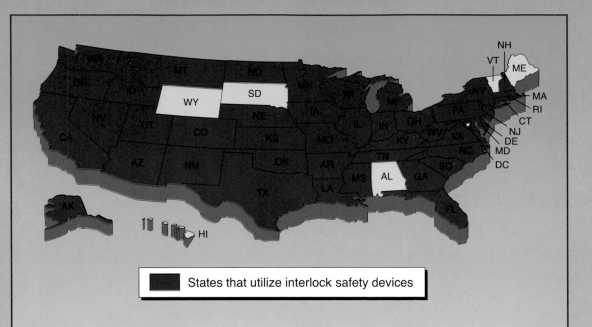

States that utilize interlock safety devices

In many states, people who have been convicted of drunk driving are required to install an interlock safety device on their car. The device is attached to the steering wheel. The driver must blow into a tube that measures the driver's blood alcohol concentration (BAC). If any alcohol is detected in the driver's breath, the car will not start.

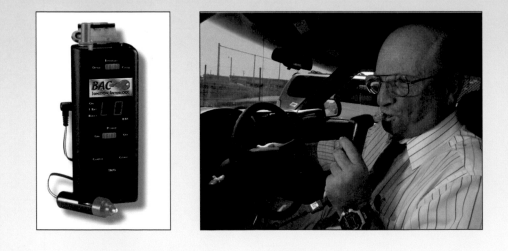

Source: Mothers Against Drunk Driving, www.madd.org.

second law mandates that juries hear all drunken driving cases. It then instructs juries to consider the evidence *"in a light most favorable to the prosecution,"* an absurd evidentiary standard at odds with everything the American criminal justice system is supposed to stand for.

Further Threats to Civil Liberties

Even scarier are the laws that didn't pass, but will inevitably be introduced again. New Mexico's state legislature nearly passed a law that would mandate ignition interlock devices on every car sold in the state beginning in 2008, regardless of the buyer's driving record. Drivers would have been required to pass a breath test to start the car, then again every 10 minutes while driving. Car computer systems would have kept records of the tests, which would have been downloaded at service centers and sent to law enforcement officials for evaluation. New York considered a similar law.

That isn't to say we ought to ease up on drunken drivers. But our laws should be grounded in sound science and the presumption of innocence, not in hysteria. They should target repeat offenders and severely impaired drunks, not social drinkers who straddle the legal threshold. Though the threat of drunken driving has significantly diminished over the last 20 years, it's still routinely overstated by anti-alcohol activists and lawmakers. Even if the threat were as severe as it's often portrayed, casting aside basic criminal protections and civil liberties is the wrong way to address it.

THREE

A Blood Alcohol Concentration Limit of .08 Saves Lives

National Highway Traffic Safety Administration

Blood alcohol concentration (BAC) is the measurement used to determine the amount of alcohol present in the bloodstream. In the following fact sheet, the National Highway Traffic Safety Administration (NHTSA) states that drivers with a BAC of .08 percent and above experience critical impairment of their driving abilities, including problems with judgment, reaction time, steering, divided attention, and lane changing. These impairments greatly increase their risk of being killed or injured in motor vehicle crashes. The NHTSA favors laws making it illegal to drive with a BAC of .08 or above. Studies have found consistent and persuasive evidence that .08 BAC laws are associated with reduced incidence of alcohol-related fatal crashes according to the NHTSA. A .08 BAC limit is reasonable and has the potential for saving hundreds of lives and reducing thousands of serious injuries each year. The National Highway Traffic Safety Administration, a division of the U.S. Department of Transportation, conducts safety programs to reduce deaths, injuries, and economic losses resulting from motor vehicle crashes.

National Highway Traffic Safety Administration, ".08 BAC Illegal *per se* Level," *Traffic Safety Facts*, vol. 2, March 2004.

It is illegal per se (in itself) to drive a motor vehicle with a blood alcohol concentration (BAC) at or above a specified level in all States. The previous level in most states had been .10 BAC for drivers 21 and older, but now 45 States, the District of Columbia, and Puerto Rico have enacted laws that set a lower level of .08 BAC. In a 1992 Report to Congress, NHTSA [National Highway Traffic Safety Administration] recommended that all States lower the illegal *per se* level to .08 for all drivers 21 and older. . . . [Editor's note: Today, all fifty states have passed .08 BAC limits. Delaware was the last state to adopt the .08 BAC in July 2004.]

A California Highway Patrol officer administers a breathalyzer test to a suspected drunk driver to determine his blood alcohol level.

About .08

- In 2002, 41 percent of the 42,815 motor vehicle deaths were alcohol-related. This translates to 17,419 alcohol-related motor vehicle deaths during that year, accounting for an average of one alcohol-related fatality every 30 minutes.
- The National Highway Traffic Safety Administration's position on the relationship between blood alcohol concentration and driving is that driving performance degrades with every drink.
- A comprehensive NHTSA study provides what is perhaps clear evidence of the significant impairment that occurs in the driving-related skills of all drivers with .08 BAC, regardless of age, gender, or drinking history.

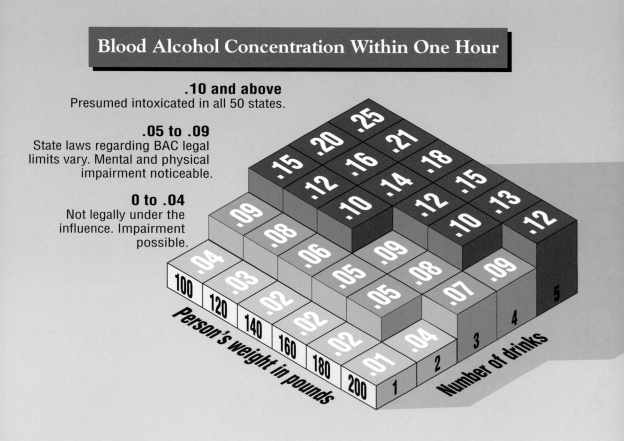

Blood Alcohol Concentration Within One Hour

.10 and above
Presumed intoxicated in all 50 states.

.05 to .09
State laws regarding BAC legal limits vary. Mental and physical impairment noticeable.

0 to .04
Not legally under the influence. Impairment possible.

Person's weight in pounds

Number of drinks

- .08 BAC laws are effective in reducing alcohol-related fatal crashes. At least 10 studies, covering many of the States that have enacted .08 BAC laws, have consistently shown that .08 BAC laws are associated with reductions in alcohol-related fatalities, particularly in conjunction with the administrative license revocation (ALR) laws that are present in 41 States.

- NHTSA has published several comprehensive studies on the effectiveness of .08 BAC laws. These studies found consistent and persuasive evidence that .08 BAC laws are associated with reduced incidence of alcohol-related fatal crashes. A study of the effectiveness of a .08 BAC law implemented in Illinois in 1997, found that the .08 BAC law was associated with a 13.7 percent decline in the number of drinking drivers involved in fatal crashes. The reduction included drivers at both high and low BAC levels. This is significant because critics of .08 BAC laws have often claimed that these laws do not affect the behavior of high BAC drivers. The study also found that there were no major problems reported by local law enforcement or court systems due to the change in the law. An updated analysis of Illinois's law estimated that 105 lives were saved in the first two calendar years since its implementation.

- In a comprehensive study of drivers involved in fatal crashes in all 50 states and DC from 1982 to 1997, it was estimated that .08 BAC laws reduced driver alcohol-related fatal crashes by 8 percent.

- A 1999 report by the U.S. General Accounting Office (GAO) reviewed the studies available at that time and found *strong indications that .08 BAC laws, in combination with other drunk driving laws (particularly license revocation laws), sustained public education and information efforts, and vigorous and consistent enforcement, can save lives.* The GAO report also concluded that a .08 (BAC) law can be *an important component of a State's overall highway safety program.*

Why .08?

The research is clear. Virtually all drivers, even those who are experienced drinkers, are significantly impaired at a .08 BAC. As early as 1988, a NHTSA review of 177 studies clearly documented this impairment. NHTSA released a later review of 112 more recent studies, providing additional evidence of impairment at .08 BAC and below. The results of the nearly 300 studies reviewed have shown that, at a .08 BAC level, virtually all drivers are impaired in the performance of critical driving tasks such as divided attention, complex reaction time, steering, lane changing, and judgment.

The risk of being in a crash gradually increases as a driver's BAC increases, but rises more rapidly once a driver reaches or exceeds .08 BAC compared to drivers with no alcohol in their blood stream. A recent study estimated that drivers at .08 to .09 BACs are anywhere from 11 to 52 times more likely to be involved in a fatal crash than drivers at .00 BAC, depending upon their age and gender.

Lowering the *per se* limit is an effective countermeasure that will reduce alcohol-related traffic fatalities, especially when combined with an ALR law. There was a 12 percent reduction in alcohol-related fatalities in California in 1990 after a .08 and an ALR law went into effect. The decrease in alcohol-related fatalities occurred at both high and low BAC levels, including drivers with BAC levels of .20 or greater. A 1996 study at Boston University showed that States adopting .08 laws experienced 16 percent and 18 percent post-law declines in the proportions of fatal crashes involving fatally-injured drivers whose BAC levels were .08 or higher and .15 or higher, respectively. The Centers for Disease Control (CDC) and Prevention concluded that .08 BAC laws are associated with a median 7 percent reduction in alcohol-related traffic fatalities in States that adopt them.

The .08 BAC limit is reasonable and has the potential for saving hundreds of lives and reducing thousands of serious injuries each year, if implemented by all States.

The public supports a .08 BAC level. A survey conducted in 2001 indicated that 88% of the people in States with .08 laws support the law.

Derailing Myths About .08

States considering .08 BAC laws should review all the facts, including the rationale behind the .08 goal and the potential impact on

The Effects of Blood Alcohol Concentration (BAC) Levels

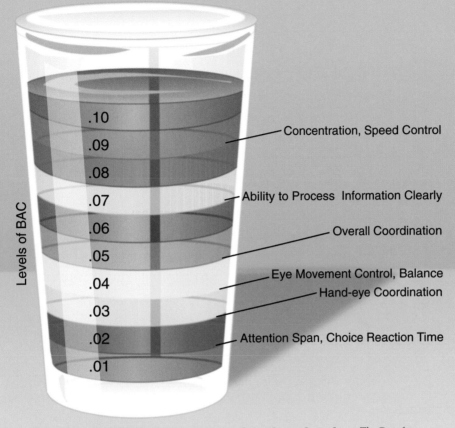

Levels of BAC

.10
.09
.08 — Concentration, Speed Control
.07 — Ability to Process Information Clearly
.06 — Overall Coordination
.05 — Eye Movement Control, Balance
.04 — Hand-eye Coordination
.03
.02 — Attention Span, Choice Reaction Time
.01

Source: National Highway Traffic Safety Administration, *Setting Limits, Saving Lives: The Case for .08 BAC Laws*, April 2001.

alcohol-related deaths. Opposition to .08 laws generally includes the following arguments:

- **Point:** In 1999, the U.S. General Accounting Office (GAO) conducted a critical review of the .08 studies and concluded that these laws are not effective in reducing alcohol-related fatalities.
- **Counterpoint:** This statement is not correct! The GAO report stated that there are *"strong indications that .08 BAC laws, in combination with other drunk driving laws (particularly license revocation laws), sustained public education and information efforts, and vigorous and consistent enforcement, can save lives."*

- **Point:** ".08 BAC legislation will not affect problem drinker drivers who have high BAC levels."
- **Counterpoint:** The latest research shows that .08 BAC laws not only reduce the incidence of impaired driving at lower BAC levels, they also reduce the incidence of impaired driving at higher BAC levels (i.e., over .10). A .08 BAC law serves as a general deterrent to all those who drink and drive because it sends a message that the State is getting tougher on impaired driving, and it makes many people think twice about getting behind the wheel after they have had too much to drink. A .08 BAC law should be a key component of any State's overall program to reduce impaired driving. While repeat offenders do account for a significant part of the problem, most fatally-injured drinking drivers have no prior alcohol-related offenses.
- **Point:** .08 BAC laws make criminals out of normal social drinkers.
- **Counterpoint:** Impairment and crash risk are the issues, not how many drinks it may take to get to a .08 BAC level. Numerous studies have indicated that at a .08 BAC level, virtually all drivers are impaired on critical driving tasks such as divided attention, complex reaction time, steering, lane changing, and judgment.

- In addition, studies have shown that the risk of being involved in a fatal crash is much greater than at a .08 BAC level.

- **Point:** ".08 is just the first step in a movement toward zero tolerance."
- **Counterpoint:** A .08 BAC limit is not meant to restrict individuals from drinking alcohol. Rather, the limit exists to prevent individuals from operating a motor vehicle while impaired by alcohol, putting their own lives, and the lives of others at risk.
- **Point:** .08 BAC laws will overwhelm police and clog the criminal justice system.
- **Counterpoint:** Two studies, one in California and another in Illinois, looked at the impact of .08 BAC laws on enforcement efforts and the criminal justice system. These studies have not

found any significant problems with the enforcement of lower BAC limits for police or the State courts.

.05 BAC Limit in Other Countries

The international trend continues to be to reduce illegal *per se* limits to .05 BAC or lower. The illegal limit is .05 BAC in numerous countries, including Australia, Belgium, Bulgaria, Denmark, Finland, France, Germany, Greece, Ireland, Israel, The Netherlands, Portugal, Russia, South Africa, Spain, and Turkey. Russia, Sweden, and Norway have a limit of .02 BAC and Poland recently went to .03 BAC. Several countries have reported studies indicating that lowering the illegal *per se* limit from .08 BAC to .05 BAC reduces alcohol-related fatalities (e.g., Australia, Austria, Belgium, The Netherlands, and France).

Laboratory studies from these countries indicate that impairment in critical driving functions begins at low BACs. Most subjects in these studies were significantly impaired at .05 BAC with regard to visual acuity, vigilance, drowsiness, psychomotor skills, and information processing, compared to their performance at .00 BAC.

Leading medical, crash prevention, public health and traffic safety organizations in the world support BAC limits at .05 or lower, including: the World Medical Association, the American and British Medical Associations, the European Commission, the European Transport Safety Council, the World Health Organization, and the American College of Emergency Physicians.

FOUR

A Blood Alcohol Concentration Limit of .08 Does Not Save Lives

Charles V. Peña

In the following excerpt Charles V. Peña writes that near-ly two-thirds of alcohol-related deaths involve drivers with a blood alcohol concentration (BAC) of .15 percent and above. The average BAC level in a fatal crash is .17 per-cent. Therefore, he contends that lowering the legal limit for BAC from .10 to .08 will not deter drunk drivers and will not reduce the number of alcohol-related deaths. He insists that studies in support of lowering the BAC to .08 are riddled with inaccuracies and have been completely refuted by the watchdog of the federal government, the General Accountability Office (GAO). The .08 BAC limit will punish responsible drinkers and do nothing to stop the real threat on America's roadways—the severely drunk drivers, Peña concludes. Furthermore, the .08 limit masks a hidden agenda on the part of anti–drunk driving groups—a push to legislate a new Prohibition. Charles V. Peña is the former executive director of the Northern Virginia Chapter of Mothers Against Drunk Driving (MADD) and the former executive director of the American Council on Alcoholism. He is currently a pol-icy studies director at the Cato Institute, a public policy think tank in Washington, D.C.

B AC, or blood alcohol content, is the measurement that determines how much alcohol an individual has in his or her bloodstream. A BAC of .06 means that your blood has a .06% blood alcohol content. BAC also serves as a quick-and-easy quantifiable measurement that allows law enforcement to define "drunk" in the context of drunk driving. In the 1990s, most states set .10% BAC as the legal limit for driving—anything over that limit and you were breaking the law.

In 1998, MADD [Mothers Against Drunk Driving] pushed Congress to withhold federal highway funds from any state that failed to lower their legal limit to .08% BAC. MADD lost the battle in Washington that year, and in the states. 1998 and 1999 saw more than 50 separate legislative sessions covering 32 states consider the

David Walker, comptroller general of the United States and head of the General Accountability Office, has criticized government studies purporting to show that .08 BAC laws save lives.

.08% BAC standard. Only Texas and Washington adopted it. But in 2000, MADD successfully reintroduced their legislation at the federal level—far away from the normal citizens whose state representatives passed hundreds of other highway-safety laws on their merits. At a high-profile White House Rose Garden event, Bill Clinton signed the .08% BAC bill into law. . . .

The battle over .08% BAC legislation glaringly illustrates how MADD has turned its attention from truly drunk drivers to drinking more generally. And how the anti–drunk driving message shifted from "friends don't let friends drive drunk" to the more radical message of "don't drink and drive."

Emergency workers attempt to extricate a driver, possibly driving under the influence, from an overturned car on a surface street.

MADD generally attempts to mask its radical, neo-prohibitionist agenda in the veneer of sound science and sober statistics. So the push to blackmail states into lowering the legal BAC level required "studies" that might provide "evidence" of reduced drunk-driving fatalities should their law pass. A few inconvenient facts stood in MADD's way. First, the U.S. Department of Transportation's Fatality Analysis Reporting System (FARS) data show that the average BAC level in a fatal crash where a driver was actually tested is .17%—more than double the proposed .08% BAC standard. Second, the typical DWI [driving while intoxicated] fatality is caused by a person who has had more than *nine drinks* before driving. And third, nearly two-thirds of alcohol-related deaths involve drivers with BACs of .15% and above. Even MADD knows that lowering the BAC to .08% BAC will have no effect on these flagrant scofflaws.

Pseudo Science

Despite the challenges introduced by reality, MADD still manages to cite studies claiming that the .08% BAC law saves lives. The most prominent of these was conducted by Boston University sociologist Ralph Hingson, who declared that a national .08% BAC law would save "500 to 600 lives a year." Even before considering its methodological flaws, the Hingson study should be considered suspect because its author—who is not a traffic safety professional—has a serious axe to grind. Hingson has a history of anti-drinking activism, has published nearly 50 manuscripts on the dangers of alcohol generally, and currently serves as MADD's Vice President of Public Policy. He is anything but an impartial researcher.

Dr. Robert Scopatz is a traffic-research scientist who directed New York City's Transportation Research Office before helping create NHTSA [National Highway Traffic Safety Administration] data-analysis programs. He reviewed the Hingson study. What did he discover?

Hingson's study paired several .10% states with "neighboring" states that had adopted .08 BAC laws. But Hingson had gone "state shopping." For example, he compared .08% BAC California with .10% BAC Texas—hardly "neighbor" states. Had Hingson compared .08% BAC California to .10% BAC Arizona, he would have found no difference between the two. Clearly, Hingson was picking and choosing his comparison states so that the results would align with his prejudices. Using the same data and number crunching techniques as Hingson, Scopatz concluded: "Selection of logically valid comparison states eliminated any evidence of an effect of the .08% BAC laws in the states that passed them." But Hingson's number crunching techniques were invalid as well. Scopatz observed Hingson's meta-analysis approach is "not commonly applied to traffic safety research."

Another study by Dr. Robert Voas estimated that "590 lives could have been saved" in 1997 if all states adopted .08% BAC laws. But Voas, like Ralph Hingson, has been a member of MADD's board of directors. And Voas works for the Pacific Institute for Research and Evaluation, which endorses a roadblock program that stops every other car at least once annually. He is anything but objective.

Aside from Hingson's flawed study, and Voas's wild assertions, opponents of drinking and driving also point to a report published by NHTSA—which increasingly marches in lock step with MADD—arguing that 500 lives would be spared every year were the .08% BAC law to pass. But in 1999, the General Accounting Office (GAO), the watchdog of the Federal Government, completely refuted NHTSA's .08% BAC study. In fact, of seven NHTSA papers the GAO reviewed, they found four that "had limitations and raised methodological concerns." Guess whose paper was included in the GAO's rebuke? That's right. Ralph Hingson's.

Other Flawed Studies

Among the NHTSA-sponsored studies admonished by the GAO was one 1991 report predicting a 12% drop in alcohol-related highway deaths in California under a .08% BAC standard. The GAO said the study failed to factor in lives saved by a new license-revocation law. . . .

Candy Lightner, the founder of Mothers Against Drunk Driving, opposes .08 BAC laws, maintaining that they fail to target hard-core drunk drivers.

Three other NHTSA-cited studies, said GAO, "fall short of conclusively establishing that .08% BAC laws by themselves have resulted in reductions in alcohol related fatalities." Specifically:

1. A 1999 NHTSA study of 11 states with .08% BAC laws concluded that just two of the 11 saw reductions in alcohol-related fatalities, while nine did not. Yet NHTSA cited the study as

"additional support for the premise that .08% BAC laws help to reduce alcohol-related fatalities"—a relationship, said the GAO, that even the study's authors "[did] not draw."

2. The GAO accused NHTSA of *suppressing its own study* concluding, "that the .08 BAC law in North Carolina had little clear effect." Disturbed by the study's failure to support the

A sign alongside an Illinois highway makes clear the state's zero tolerance of drivers whose BAC exceeds the .08 legal limit.

proposition that .08% BAC saved lives, NHTSA asked its author, Dr. Robert Foss, to recalculate. "We looked real hard [for] measurable effects of this law," said the scientist. "Try as we might, we didn't find anything." NHTSA then waited 13 months to unveil Foss' report, only to pass it off as *supporting* the agency's .08% BAC position.

3. GAO dismissed a 1999, 50-state NHTSA study for using flawed methodology. They chose an analytical method apt to produce a "numerical effect that is larger than other methods." In common parlance, that's called exaggeration.

Considering all the pseudo science employed by NHTSA, the GAO concluded:

> [T]he evidence does not conclusively establish that .08 BAC laws by themselves result in reductions in the number and severity of crashes involving alcohol. . . . NHTSA's position—that the evidence was conclusive—was overstated."

Dismissing the conclusions of its own authors, willfully employing flawed methodology, and selectively publicizing misleading information. That's the NHTSA, which—in its zeal to promote MADD-inspired legislation—improperly places the imprimatur of a supposedly neutral government agency on junk science.

NHTSA can no longer be considered an impartial arbiter of the nation's accident statistics. . . .

.08% BAC Despite the Facts

Undeterred by the many problems with the 17,448 figure, the director of NHTSA's data compilation center confidently claims that all these highway deaths would have been prevented if no driver had consumed any alcohol. Never mind the nearly 2,000 drunk pedestrians who got themselves killed. NHTSA is less concerned with accuracy than with achieving its agenda.

The more evidence that comes in from states that have gone to a .08% BAC standard, the weaker the case is for .08. In a fair fight of facts, the argument for .08% BAC lost again and again:

- Of the first 13 states that dropped their BAC threshold to .08% BAC, 46% saw alcohol-related fatality *increase* in one of the first two years thereafter. The logical inference: it's even money whether death rates will drop or rise post-.08, because the standard is safety-neutral.
- A December 1998 report to the New Jersey Senate—written by a blue-ribbon task force including police officers, judges, clergy members, and doctors—found that "the impact of [.08 laws] is inconclusive."
- Even .08% BAC advocate Voas wrote, "drivers in the .08 to .09 range . . . often do not exhibit the blatant erratic driving of higher BAC offenders." Could this be because they are not dangerous?

Statistics like these compel Tom Rukavina, a state legislator from Minnesota, to deny any safety benefit from a .08 law. He estimates that the law would merely result in 6,000 additional criminal arrests in Minnesota, costing the public sixty million dollars. . . .

Focus on Drunk Driving, Not Drinking

I worry that the movement I helped create has lost direction. [.08 legislation] ignores the real core of the problem. . . . If we really want to save lives, let's go after the most dangerous drivers on the road.
—Candy Lightner, founder of MADD

What is to be done? We must unmask the true menace—the chronic, ungovernable drunk driver who is not deterred by drunk driving laws of any kind. Political and financial resources being finite, it's imperative not to spend them chasing responsible social drinkers just to keep special interest groups in business.

Even MADD occasionally shows signs of understanding the real problem when it comes to drunk driving. In late 1999, it launched a nationwide offensive against "repeat offenders and super-drunk drivers." In a press release, it cited NHTSA data that spotlighted, for once, the real problem. According to NHTSA, two-thirds of all alcohol-related highway deaths implicate drivers with a BAC level of .15% or higher. Indeed, the driver who killed MADD founder Candy Lightner's daughter had a .20% BAC. And the killer of former MADD President Karolyn Nunnallee's child registered .24% BAC. Too bad MADD generally ignores the evidence that strikes closest to home.

Even when public attitudes toward drinking and driving were highly permissive, the "super-drunk driver" with an alcohol addiction has been the overarching threat. According to Voas, approximately one-half of first-time DWI offenders have BAC of at least 0.15% when arrested. A nationwide pre-trial screening service discovered that more than 70% of repeat drunk-driving offenders were hard-core alcoholics, with an average BAC of .20%.

The driving peril of high-BAC drivers who cause the lion's share of alcohol-linked highway deaths will remain undiminished as long as law-enforcement energies focus on the wrong target: low BAC drivers. Ever-lower BAC standards, as the 1995 California DMV study of that state's .08% BAC law concluded, merely cause in-control drinkers to further restrict their intake before driving. The alcoholic scofflaw keeps on drinking to the max.

Graduated Penalties Are Needed

States that allow on-the-spot administrative driver's license suspensions, that aggressively enforce sensible BAC limits, and that strongly penalize convicted drunk drivers who continue to drive on suspended licenses are pursuing strategies that really get potential killers off the road. What's missing, however, is a system of graduated penalties. Every state in the nation employs such a system for speeding—fining, for example, the driver who exceeds the speed limit by 40 mph substantially more than the one who goes 10 mph over the limit. Only recently have states begun to acknowledge the need for increased penalties for high-BAC drivers, but these levels generally start at twice the federal mandate of .08% BAC. In most states, however, stay just this side of your state's BAC and you are (generally) unpunished. Go one-hundredth of one percent over the line and endure the same sanctions that await a serious drunk driver.

The result? Society recoils from legislating the kind of sanctions that truly drunk drivers deserve, lest they be forced to apply overly-harsh punishments to technical violators of BAC laws. Even NHTSA admits that a 120-pound woman with an average metabolism will hit .08% BAC if she drinks two six-ounce glasses of wine over the course of two hours. Common sense says she shouldn't go to jail for getting behind the wheel.

Penalties for repeat offenders should be substantially harsher, with prison terms—hard time—awaiting drunk drivers who drive on a suspended license. Truly drunk driving *is* a crime. It's time we began applying the same punishment paradigm to that offense that governs all others.

MADD's founder is right: "If we really want to save lives, let's go after the most dangerous drivers on the road." Marshaling public support for this goal would be the first step in seeing a dramatic decrease in the toll of drunk driving's victims.

FIVE

Roadblocks Stop Drunk Drivers

Jeffrey W. Greene

In the following article Jeffrey W. Greene writes that sobriety checkpoints and saturation patrols are two effective methods of reducing the number of drunk drivers on the road. Sobriety checkpoints are used by officers to restrict traffic flow in a specific location so they can check vehicles for drunk drivers. In several states, roadblocks have reduced the annual number of alcohol-related crashes, the author notes. Saturation patrols are characterized by an increase in law enforcement officers who patrol a given geographic area, making a concentrated effort to arrest drunk drivers. Evidence shows that these patrols lead to more DUI arrests than roadblocks, Greene reports. However, roadblocks are extremely effective in their own respect because they increase public awareness that drunk drivers will be caught, arrested, and punished. Jeffrey W. Greene is a freelance writer who contributes to the *FBI Law Enforcement Bulletin*.

Law enforcement has two basic methods of dealing with the DUI [driving under the influence] problem—sobriety checkpoints and saturation patrols. Sobriety checkpoints have existed for several years and have served as a deterrent to drunk driving across many communities. Although not the most aggressive

Jeffrey W. Greene, "Battling DUI: A Comparative Analysis of Checkpoints and Saturation Patrols," *FBI Law Enforcement Bulletin*, vol. 72, January 2003.

method of removing impaired drivers from America's roadways, these checkpoints comprise one piece of public awareness and education relevant to the drinking and driving dilemma.

Saturation patrols, on the other hand, constitute a vigorous tactic employed by law enforcement agencies to significantly impact an area known for a high concentration of alcohol-impaired drivers. Law enforcement agencies have used saturation patrols much longer than checkpoints, sometimes under a different name or no name at all. Which method offers the best use of law enforcement's limited resources? The choice depends upon many issues, such as funding, resource allocations, and targeted areas.

A highway patrol officer tests a driver during a sobriety checkpoint. Officers set up checkpoints in areas where a large number of alcohol-related crashes or offenses occur.

The Problem

According to National Highway Traffic Safety Administration statistics, 16,653 people died in alcohol-related crashes in 2000, an increase of more than 800 deaths from 1999. This represented the largest percentage increase on record. By some estimates, about two out of every five Americans will be involved in an alcohol-related crash at some time in their lives. These tragic statistics dramatically illustrate that DUI is a serious problem.

Research has indicated, however, that most impaired drivers never get arrested. Police stop some drivers, but often miss signs of impairment. Estimates revealed that as many as 2,000 alcohol-impaired driving trips occur for every arrest, and, even when special drinking-driving enforcement patrols are conducted, as many as 300 trips occur for each arrest. Because the police cannot catch all offenders, the success of alcohol-impaired driving laws depends on deterring potential offenders by creating the public perception that apprehension and punishment of offenders is probable. Research also has shown that the likelihood of apprehension is more important in deterring offenders than the severity of punishment. Therefore, enforcement is the key to creating the perception of a possibility of capture, while publicizing these efforts can effect a real threat of detainment.

Sobriety Checkpoints

Sobriety checkpoint programs are defined as procedures in which law enforcement officers restrict traffic flow in a designated, specific location so they can check drivers for signs of alcohol impairment. If officers detect any type of incapacitation based upon their observations, they can perform additional testing, such as field sobriety or breath analysis tests. To this end, agencies using checkpoints must have a written policy as a directive for their officers to follow.

Agencies normally choose locations for checkpoints from areas that statistically reveal a large number of alcohol-related crashes or offenses. Officers stop vehicles based on traffic flow, staffing, and overall safety. They must stop vehicles in an arbitrary sequence, whether they stop all vehicles or a specified portion of them. Checkpoints offer a visible enforcement method intended to deter potential offenders, as well as to apprehend impaired drivers. Agencies should set up checkpoints frequently, over extended periods, and publicize them well.

Sobriety checkpoints must display warning signs to approaching motorists. Also, they normally will provide opportunities for drivers to actually avoid the checkpoint, usually with an alternate route that a driver could divert to after passing the checkpoint warning signs. Agencies typically post an officer in a marked cruiser at each end of the checkpoint. These officers can observe the driving behavior of those who choose to avoid the checkpoint.

Used to deter drinking and driving, sobriety checkpoints are related more directly to educating the public and encouraging designated drivers, rather than actually apprehending impaired drivers. Typically, sobriety checkpoints do not yield a large volume of DUI arrests. Instead, they offer authorities an educational tool. Education and awareness serve as a significant part of deterrence. Frequent use of checkpoints and aggressive media coverage can create a convincing threat in people's minds that officers *will* apprehend impaired drivers—a key to general deterrence. In addition, public opinion polls have indicated that 70 to 80 percent of Americans surveyed favored the increased use of sobriety checkpoints as an effective law enforcement tool to combat impaired driving.

Saturation Patrols

Saturation patrols involve an increased enforcement effort targeting a specific geographic area to identify and arrest impaired drivers. This area always is much larger than the location chosen for a sobriety checkpoint. However, site selection proves vital in both sobriety checkpoints and saturation patrol initiatives. Some states require documentation as to why a specific location was chosen. Selected sites should have a statistically high incidence of DUI crashes or fatalities and take into account officer and motorist safety.

Saturation patrols, in which police focus on identifying drunk drivers in a particular area, may be more effective than sobriety checkpoints.

Saturation patrols concentrate their enforcement on impaired driving behaviors, such as left of center, following too closely, reckless driving, aggressive driving, and speeding. Multiple agencies often combine and concentrate their resources to conduct saturation patrols. Therefore, planning represents a vital part of these efforts. All involved parties should participate in the planning phase, furnishing their specific views and concerns.

Saturation patrols may afford a more effective means of detecting repeat offenders, who are likely to avoid detection at sobriety checkpoints. These patrols also may more effectively impact a specific geographic location with a history of a high number of alcohol-related crashes. They must enhance people's perceptions of being detected to be effective. Therefore, saturation patrols require the same intense media attention as sobriety checkpoints. In addition, prosecutors and judges must support saturation patrols. These efforts also must remain ongoing, not merely a onetime operation, to produce successful results, the same as with sobriety checkpoint programs.

A Comparative Study

Statistics compiled by two agencies, similar in size and area of responsibility, offer an overview of the scope of the DUI problem.

San Francisco police officers check for drunk drivers in a long line of cars at a sobriety checkpoint on Christmas in 2004.

In 2000, the Missouri State Highway Patrol conducted 58 sobriety checkpoints and arrested 323 drivers for DUI. The Ohio State Highway Patrol carried out 12 sobriety checkpoints and arrested 77 drivers for DUI. In 2001, Missouri effected 67 sobriety checkpoints and arrested 318 drivers for DUI. Ohio implemented 19 sobriety checkpoints and arrested 126 drivers for DUI. Since 1989, the Ohio State Highway Patrol has participated in 156 sobriety checkpoints and arrested 807 drivers for DUI.

In the past 2 years [prior to January 2003], the Missouri State Highway Patrol conducted 822 saturation patrol operations, arresting 1,666 drivers for DUI. The Ohio State Highway Patrol performs saturation patrols on a regular basis across the state. The agency arrests an average of 25,000 DUI drivers per year through all DUI-related operations.

In another example, from 1994 to 1995, Tennessee, in cooperation with the National Highway Traffic Safety Administration, implemented a statewide campaign completing nearly 900 sobriety checkpoints. Law enforcement agencies conducted these in all 95 counties in Tennessee in just over 1 year. The checkpoint program was highly publicized and conducted basically every week. The evaluation of the program revealed it as highly favorable in reducing the number of alcohol-related fatal crashes. Although the program only netted 773 arrests for DUI, the deterrent factor created by the continuous use of the checkpoints and the media attention received resulted in the program's success. What do these statistics convey? Basically, Missouri averaged about five DUI arrests per checkpoint, Ohio averaged less than seven DUI arrests per checkpoint, and Tennessee's aggressive checkpoint program averaged less than one DUI arrest per checkpoint. What these figures do not show is the number of impaired drivers deterred by the operations, either through sobriety checkpoints or saturation patrols. Those statistics never will be clearly identified, but *any* lives saved by such efforts are worth the effort and resources allocated.

What also is not accounted for in these statistics is the additional number of other enforcement actions taken, such as safety belt, commercial vehicle, and child safety seat arrests; speeding violations; warnings for various traffic infractions or vehicle

Handelsman. © 2005 by knight Ridder/Tribune Information Services. Reproduced by permission.

defects; and motorist assists. Detecting such additional violations is more probable during saturation patrols, as opposed to sobriety checkpoints. This alone could represent another measure of effectiveness of saturation patrols.

Overall, measured in arrests per hour, a dedicated saturation patrol is the most effective method of apprehending offenders. Such concerted efforts also may serve as a general deterrence if their activities are publicized and become widely known.

Critics have pointed out that sobriety checkpoints produce fewer arrests per hour than dedicated patrols, but some studies show arrest rates can be increased greatly when police employ passive alcohol sensors (i.e., devices that can measure the alcohol content in the air, which officers can use while talking to a motorist passing through the checkpoint) to help detect drinking drivers. However, focusing on arrests is a misleading way to consider the value of checkpoints. The purpose of frequent checkpoints is to increase public awareness and deter potential offenders, resulting in the ideal situation where very few offenders are left to apprehend.

Sobriety checkpoint programs in Florida, North Carolina, New Jersey, Tennessee, and Virginia have led to a reduction in alcohol-related crashes. In 1995, North Carolina conducted a statewide enforcement and publicity campaign aimed at impaired drivers. The campaign was deemed a success, indicating "drivers with blood alcohol levels at or above 0.08 percent declined from 198 per 10,000 before the program to 90 per 10,000 after the intensive 3-week alcohol-impaired publicity and enforcement campaign."

The Importance of Public Awareness

Is public awareness and education important? The key aspect in both sobriety checkpoints and saturation patrols rests with public awareness. The perception of a higher risk of detection for driving under the influence of alcohol may deter more people from driving after drinking. The more the public understands the issues and severity of the consequences, the better they will accept drunk driving as a problem and will embrace a crusade to reduce occurrences. Indeed, agencies must have public support to succeed.

All law enforcement agencies must accept that the media plays a vital role in combating impaired drivers. They must use all outlets possible to spread the word about this needless tragedy that happens every day. All media entities are looking for stories. By working closely with them, agencies can get the message out about the dangers of drunk driving. The sooner agencies realize the importance of the media, the sooner they will gain a valuable ally in their fight. Agencies can garner a great deal of support from the public when they speak out on this vital issue.

Are stricter laws and sanctions working? Twenty-seven states and the District of Columbia have reduced their blood alcohol content (BAC) threshold to .08 percent from .10 percent in another effort to reduce the number of alcohol-related crashes. The federal government also has adopted the standard of .08 percent BAC, encouraging states to change to .08 percent. In 2003, states that have not adopted the .08 percent standard will lose millions of federal dollars for road construction. Currently, 22 states have the BAC threshold of .10 percent, Ohio included. Studies by the

Centers for Disease Control and Prevention's National Center for Injury Prevention and Control indicated, on average, that states adopting .08 percent have reduced crash deaths involving alcohol by 7 percent. [Editor's note: Today, all fifty states have passed .08 BAC limits. Delaware was the last state to adopt the .08 BAC in July 2004.]

Administrative license suspension laws continue to become more aggressive, attempting to create a stronger deterrent environment. Estimates have indicated that they reduce driver involvement in fatal crashes by about 9 percent. Some laws providing for the suspension or revocation of licenses have indicated a reduction in the subsequent crash involvement of those drivers who previously have been convicted of an alcohol-related offense. Although it is known that many suspended drivers continue to drive, they tend to drive less and possibly more carefully, attempting to avoid detection.

Recommendations

While many conclusions can be drawn from an analysis of sobriety checkpoints and saturation patrols, both serve a significant purpose and, used together, can be effective in reducing the number of impaired drivers. Law enforcement agencies may find that only one of these works for them, depending upon resources. Others may determine a combination of both is needed to successfully combat the problem in their communities. Regardless of the selected method, it remains essential to identify the specific keys to removing more impaired drivers from U.S. highways, including—

- exposing a sufficient number of motorists to the enforcement efforts and the likelihood of being arrested;
- improving officers' skills in detecting impaired drivers;
- implementing an aggressive, continuous, and committed media effort;
- continuing efforts by legislatures and courts in an attempt to consistently punish violators and deter impaired driving; and
- identifying problem areas, high-level crash locations, and large volumes of impaired drivers.

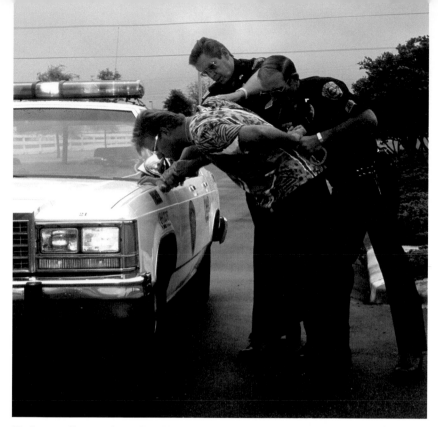

Police officers handcuff a young man after he failed a sobriety test at a checkpoint on a highway.

It is proven that saturation efforts will bring more DUI arrests than sobriety checkpoints. If that represents an agency's goal and it has the resources, then it should use saturation patrols. If an agency's goal weighs heavier on the educational side, it should use sobriety checkpoints. If an agency should choose to use checkpoints over saturation patrols, the evidence is clear that infrequent use is not effective. So, an agency must consider the cost incurred with the frequent use of sobriety checkpoints. Resources (time and money) may greatly affect an agency's decision regarding which method to employ.

If an agency's goal is to reduce the number of impaired drivers over time, it should use both sobriety checkpoints and saturation patrols, as well as any other available methods. The bottom line is to do something—do everything—to remove impaired drivers from America's highways.

SIX

Roadblocks Target Responsible Adults

American Beverage Institute

> In the following position paper, the American Beverage Institute (ABI) argues that roadblocks, or sobriety checkpoints, are ineffective, yielding very few drunk driving arrests. Studies have shown that properly staffed random patrols catch drunk drivers more effectively, the ABI insists. In fact, the real purpose of roadblocks is not to stop drunk drivers but to scare responsible adults with the possibility of being arrested if they enjoy a drink over dinner. The ABI concludes that roadblocks are just one scare tactic used by Mothers Against Drunk Driving (MADD) and the National Highway Traffic Safety Administration to reinforce the erroneous belief that there is no such thing as responsible drinking. The American Beverage Institute is an organization dedicated to the protection of responsible on-premise consumption of alcoholic beverages.

Roadblocks subvert existing BAC [blood alcohol concentration] laws. Drivers—and even many cops—don't understand that it is legal to drink responsibly and then drive. Most drivers believe that a police officer who finds them behind the wheel having drunk *anything at all* will impound their car and toss them in jail.

And why shouldn't normal people believe that? It's the central message of a neo-prohibitionist PR campaign conceived by MADD [Mothers Against Drunk Driving] and implemented by the National Highway Traffic Safety Administration (NHTSA), the Comprehensive Accident RAPID Evaluation (CARE) program, and other authorities. "We will not allow a man or woman to leave [a roadblock] knowing they consumed alcohol," said William Berger, former president of the International Association of Chiefs of Police. He made that comment at a press conference heralding the nationwide deployment of roadblocks as part of NHTSA's campaign entitled: "You Drink and Drive. You Lose" (YDDYL).

"Zero tolerance means zero chances," screams NHTSA in its YDDYL public relations campaign, intentionally blurring the line

The American Beverage Institute argues that adults can drink alcohol responsibly.

between legal and illegal drinking and driving. "Impaired driving is no accident. It is a violent crime that kills," said former U.S. Transportation Secretary Rodney Slater. And as we've all heard a thousand times, "impairment begins with the first drink."

NHTSA's message: if you don't want to commit a "violent crime," you need a designated driver to have a drink with dinner.

Roadblocks are not aimed at drunk drivers. Properly staffed random patrols can catch them more effectively.

Roadblocks are aimed at casual drinkers. They are meant to frighten responsible adults out of enjoying a drink over dinner at a restaurant. As MADD states on its website: "Because of the heightened visibility checkpoints give to DWI [driving while intoxicated] law enforcement, they are especially valuable and

States with Sobriety Checkpoints

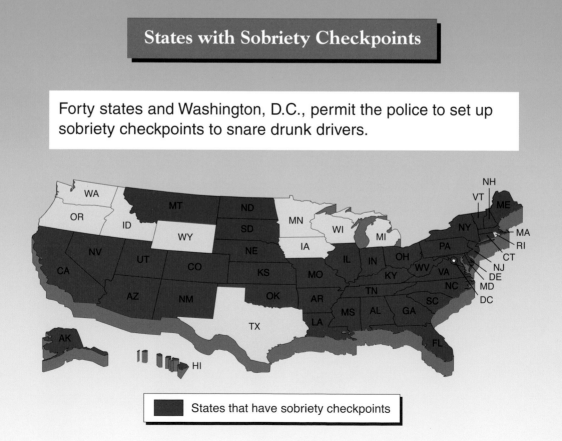

Forty states and Washington, D.C., permit the police to set up sobriety checkpoints to snare drunk drivers.

States that have sobriety checkpoints

Source: Mothers Against Drunk Driving, www.madd.org.

effective as a general deterrent. . . . If the public is aware the police will be conducting checkpoints . . . they drink less." And that's MADD's goal now—to decrease per capita consumption of adult beverages.

Rolling out a nationwide arsenal of random roadblocks would essentially prohibit alcohol consumption at many places where it is now a part of life. Imagine no beer at the ballpark, no wine with an anniversary dinner, and no champagne toasts at a wedding reception.

MADD realizes that ubiquitous roadblocks will not only scare social drinkers in the short term, but also change the culture of drinking in the long term. As average people acclimate to the fear of being arrested at roadblocks, they will refuse to drink *anything* before driving. . . .

The Real Purpose of Roadblocks

Far from the worthwhile goal of catching dangerous drunks, roadblocks have their greatest impact on the behavior of individuals who generally restrict their alcohol consumption before driving anyway.

But what do drivers have to fear? If .08 is the law, most people can have a beer with dinner and be safe even if they hit a roadblock on the way home, right?

Wrong. Even the police do not necessarily know the law. "Once you consume that alcohol," one Phoenix police detective says, "you are now a criminal because it's against the law to drink and drive. Period."

MADD and NHTSA don't want police (or the public) to know that driving with a BAC under .05% is 100 percent legal in all 50 states. Otherwise, they would know that there's no law supporting the arrest of someone who drives after enjoying a beer at the ballpark. At least not yet.

Drunk drivers can be spotted and arrested by patrol cars. Roadblocks have another purpose: to reinforce MADD's belief that there is no such thing as responsible drinking. Roadblocks are intended to terrify casual drinkers—no matter how moderately, how responsibly, how legally, or how *safely* they drink.

Stigmatizing Responsible Drinking

Roadblocks discourage social drinking because normal people simply don't understand that it is legal to drink and drive. Why the confusion? You don't have to look any further than Mothers Against Drunk Driving:

> "There is no safe blood alcohol level, and for that reason responsible drinking means no drinking and driving."
>
> —Former MADD president Katherine Prescott

> "We don't want to overlook the casual drinker. If you choose to drink you should never drive. We will not tolerate drinking and driving—period."
>
> —Former MADD president Karolyn Nunnallee

> "Impairment begins with the first drink. . . . Why take a chance? Get a designated driver."
>
> —Karolyn Nunnallee

> "It's not okay to put keys in the car when you've been drinking, forget the limits on BAC. It's just not acceptable to drink and drive. Period."
>
> —MADD fundraising letter

Of course, NHTSA is in perfect agreement with MADD. In the last days of the debate in Congress over the .08% BAC issue, the U.S. Department of Transportation released a report, "Driver Characteristics and Impairment at Various BACs," which concludes: "[A] majority of the driving population is impaired in some important measures at BACs as low as 0.02% BAC."

The report found that "by 0.04% BAC, all measures of impairment that are statistically significant are in the direction of degraded performance. The data provides no evidence of a BAC below which impairment does not occur." And finally: "the overwhelm-

A young man attempts to walk a straight line as a police officer watches him carefully for signs of intoxication.

ing majority of [research subjects] were significantly impaired by alcohol on some important measures beginning at 0.02% BAC."

Last June [2003], NHTSA released its "second installment of the YDDYL Law Enforcement Kit," which teaches communities how to establish their own sobriety checkpoints. The report stresses that "checkpoints and patrols increase the perceived risk of arrest if they are adequately publicized." Among the many publicity tactics NHTSA recommends are radio ads.

Two sample ads include these messages:

- "Impairment starts with the first drink, whether you feel it or not. Drunk driving is no accident. It's a deadly crime."
- "Designate a sober driver or one will be appointed for you . . . straight to jail. Impairment starts with the first drink, whether you feel it or not."

Law enforcement is echoing these messages all over the country. The worst part is that police actually believe what NHTSA is telling them. *Washingtonian* magazine asked two Washington, DC cops to administer breathalyzer tests to its staff. "Five of our seven staffers were candidates for arrest at BACs of .05 or .06," the magazine wrote. And one employee "wobbled" after only a single beer, so he would have been arrested as well.

A police officer at a sobriety checkpoint in San Francisco requires a suspected drunk driver to tilt his head back and touch his nose with his eyes closed.

State-level authorities also blur the line between drunk driving and legal, moderate drinking and driving. California's official guide to DUI laws is called "None For the Road." Virginia runs a high-profile program with the same name. South Carolina runs a campaign called "Operation SOS—Sober or Slammer."

Targeting Casual Drinkers

Just as terrorists know they don't need to target everyone to inspire general panic, neo-prohibitionists know they don't need to arrest everybody who drinks and drives. All they have to do is arrest a few people and publicize those arrests. That publicity generates a "chilling effect," resulting in fewer people who drink and drive.

Robert Voas, a former MADD board member and a senior researcher at PIRE [Pacific Institute for Research and Evaluation] suggests that drivers just above .08% BAC "often do not exhibit blatant erratic driving of higher BAC offenders, so the evidence of probable cause may not be present for stopping a vehicle."

Voas, of course, does not reach the obvious conclusion—that these are safe drivers. Instead, he turns it into an argument for roadblocks. How else will police catch these seemingly safe drivers? To that effect, PIRE endorses stopping at least half the U.S. driving population each year. That's more than 93.6 million drivers—nearly 2 million a week—pulled over without cause.

PIRE's staff also includes anti-alcohol stalwart James Fell, formerly of NHTSA and now on MADD's board. He argues: "Sobriety checkpoints probably are the most effective enforcement strategy we can use against alcohol impaired driving." Notice his use of the term "impaired driving"—which PIRE and MADD argue begins with the first drink.

The rhetoric of NHTSA and PIRE has real-world consequences. Their research and talking points are repeated by police chiefs, district attorneys and other authorities (not to mention reporters, public health professionals and activists).

Here's one member of the Utah House of Representatives: "A lower legal limit is an effective deterrent, especially when coupled with increased random sobriety checkpoints, because they would create the perception that, 'If I drink and drive I will be caught and punished' [which] sends a clear and rational message that there is no safe BAC limit, that impairment begins with the first drink."

MADD argues that "opponents of sobriety checkpoints tend to be those who drink and drive frequently and are concerned about being caught." That's an *ad hominem* attack which doesn't even begin to take seriously the many reasonable objections to roadblocks. Even so, MADD could be right. Most adults enjoy alcoholic beverages, and sometimes drive after consuming them in moderation.

Roadblocks Are Not Effective

A National Academy of Sciences study conducted by Jack Porter, a Harvard University economics professor, and Steven D. Levitt, a University of Chicago economics professor, concluded that roadblocks are less effective than increased general surveillance.

"Our results suggest that policies focused on stopping erratic drivers with greater frequency might be more successful," wrote Levitt and Porter in the *Journal of Political Economy*. They point out that drivers can make U-turns or refuse to take a breathalyzer test, making roadblocks less-effective strategies.

Although the Centers for Disease Control and Prevention has endorsed roadblocks, it concluded that requiring every driver who passes through a roadblock to have a breath test was no more effective than only testing drivers who looked drunk. *In other words, police discretion works.* Officers need not review every driver.

A NHTSA study on the efficacy of four roadblocks found that "only one of the checkpoints . . . was associated with a statistically significant decrease" in alcohol-related crashes. The authors note that "for chronic drunk drivers, checkpoints may not be very effective since these drivers are more likely to avoid them in the first place, and have learned to alter their driving behavior to avoid detection." They also suggest that "specific deterrence strategies, such as Roving Patrols, might be the optimum means for targeting this population of drinking drivers."

Even the IIHS [Insurance Institute for Highway Safety], which supports roadblocks, admits that they fail to yield as many arrests as random patrols: "Police prefer to conduct regular patrols rather than checkpoints because patrols may yield more arrests." And: "Officials in some of these states [that don't conduct roadblocks] say checkpoints aren't conducted more frequently because police view regular patrols as more productive."

The FBI has much to say on the subject:

- "Saturation patrols may afford a more effective means of detecting repeat offenders, who are likely to avoid detection at sobriety checkpoints."
- "Overall, measured in arrests per hour, a dedicated saturation patrol is the most effective method of apprehending offenders."
- "It is proven that saturation efforts will bring more DUI arrests than sobriety checkpoints."
- "From 1994 to 1995, Tennessee, in cooperation with the National Highway Traffic Safety Administration, implemented a statewide campaign completing nearly 900 sobriety checkpoints . . . the program only netted 773 arrests for DUI."

How do supporters defend roadblocks against the charge that they are simply not effective? They redefine "effective."

"Sobriety checkpoints are effective because they send a strong signal to the community that impaired driving will not be tolerated," said Police Chief William Berger. Prince George's County Police Capt. David Mitchell echoes his thought: "It doesn't matter that we don't make that many arrests. That's not the point."

Anti-alcohol forces have another trick up their sleeve to make roadblocks appear effective. At Alcohol Policy Conference XII, one workshop suggested: "Re-evaluate methods for measuring the effectiveness ratio of checkpoints. Use the number of people exposed to a police officer's review as the denominator as opposed to number of arrests per stops made." In other words, *pretend that roadblocks don't stop as many people as they actually do* in order to make the numbers look better.

The numbers don't look very good, after all. Even on weekend nights, police rarely arrest more than 1 percent of drivers—and some of those are surely under .08 BAC.

SEVEN

The Legal Drinking Age Should Be Enforced

Laurie Davies

> In 1984 Mothers Against Drunk Driving (MADD) led the charge to raise the minimum legal drinking age to twenty-one. In the two decades the law has been in effect, Laurie Davies reports in the following article, the National Highway Traffic Safety Administration (NHTSA) estimates that twenty thousand lives have been saved in alcohol-related crashes—more than one thousand lives a year. In contrast, when states lowered their minimum drinking age in the 1970s, Davis notes, alcohol-related teen car crashes increased by 15 to 20 percent. The author insists that despite the success of the "21" law, there is still work to be done. She contends that the government needs to establish a federal agency to deal with all underage drinking issues, including enforcing current laws and making sure underage drinkers do not have easy access to alcohol. Laurie Davies is a freelance journalist who contributes to *Driven* magazine, published by MADD.

The summer of 1984 had all the ingredients of high political drama on Capitol Hill. A young grassroots organization called MADD [Mothers Against Drunk Driving] took on the Washington political machine. And won.

At issue was the 21 minimum drinking age. Health researchers, traffic safety experts and spirited mothers who formed MADD were for it. The alcohol industry, politicians tied to the alcohol industry and restaurant owners were against it.

President Ronald Reagan—a champion of states' rights—was thought to be opposed to "21" on the grounds that the federal government should not impose a drinking age on the states.

In the end, public health won out.

This summer [in 2004], "21" turns 20 years old, and those who made it happen look back. From North Carolina Senator Elizabeth Dole's firsthand account of Oval Office discussions and New Jersey Senator Frank Lautenberg's recollection of his teenage children not speaking to him to the door-to-door visits MADD and a CBS News camera crew paid to senators' offices on the Hill, it was a colorful summer indeed.

"Today, 20,000 kids are still living because of that life-changing law," says MADD National President Wendy J. Hamilton. "But we can't put the period there. Alcohol is still the No. 1 drug for today's youth."

Contrary to the intent of the federal 21 drinking age law, loopholes in some states actually make it legal for underage drinkers to purchase, possess or consume alcohol. And people or establishments who sell or supply alcohol often receive a slap on the wrist—if any punishment at all.

Twenty years, 20,000 lives. It's a magnificent milestone. But it's not just time to look back. It's time to "fix 21."

The Deadly Data

The history of "21" really begins with the repeal of Prohibition in 1933, when nearly all of the states set 21 as the minimum legal drinking age. It was not until 1970—the same year Congress lowered the voting age to 18—that a move to lower the legal drinking age began.

"This was the Vietnam era, and the voting age had just been lowered. The argument became: If 18-year-olds can fight and vote, then they should be able to have a drink," says Alex Wagenaar,

Ph.D., professor of epidemiology at the University of Minnesota School of Public Health.

Between 1970 and 1975, 29 states lowered their minimum drinking ages. Meanwhile, 13 states kept the legal age at 21. The results of this controlled experiment were as convincing as they were tragic.

"In states that lowered the age, we found a 15 to 20 percent increase in alcohol-related teen car crashes," says Wagenaar, whose research, particularly in Michigan, helped shape the national debate.

Michigan had lowered its drinking age to 18 in 1972, then raised it back to 21 in 1978 in response to the rise in traffic crashes among 18- to 20-year-olds. Once the 21 age was restored, Wagenaar found that alcohol-involved highway crashes immediately declined in this age group.

His findings—presented two months before Michigan voters were to consider a state constitutional amendment to re-lower the drinking age from 21 to 19—made national front-page news.

"Some people did not like the news that lives were being saved," Wagenaar says. "One representative in Michigan called me a fascist. Others said the data were all cooked and this was part of a conspiracy. But I didn't bow to pressure or wonder if what I was doing was right. I was just a health scientist doing research."

Taking on Congress

As in Michigan, some states had restored the legal drinking age to 21. Yet many states held out—creating a checkerboard of state laws.

"We made a push state by state to pass '21' on its merits. But it was clear that every one of the holdout states was going to put up a difficult fight given the virulent opposition of the alcohol industry," says Chuck Hurley, who was then the lobbyist for the National Safety Council.

MADD took the battle to Washington, D.C., where newly elected President Reagan called for a special commission on drunk driving. Two years later, a top commission recommendation, led by future Illinois Gov. Jim Edgar, presented a challenge for "Mr. States' Rights," as Reagan was known. It was a proposal to deny highway funds to states that did not raise the drinking age to 21.

Supporters of MADD attend a news conference in Washington, D.C. In 1984 the organization successfully fought to raise the minimum legal drinking age to twenty-one.

"One big break came with New Jersey Congressman Jim Howard, then the chairman of the House Public Works and Transportation Committee," says Hurley, who is now a vice president with the National Safety Council.

"He held the purse strings to $75 billion for roads, bridges and dams. He literally kept a black book, and if you voted against him, you weren't going to get a project in your district for 100 years,"

Hurley jokes, remembering the day he asked Howard to introduce a bill tying highway funds to "21."

"His first question was, 'Chuck, how do the mothers feel?' That is really the endearing way he thought of MADD. And I said, 'Mr. Chairman, they're for it.'

"'Then I'm for it too,' Howard said. It was really that simple," Hurley recalls.

The Howard bill passed the House on a voice vote.

In the Senate, New Jersey freshman Senator Frank Lautenberg tacked similar legislation onto the Senate highway bill. "Between New York, where the drinking age was 18, and New Jersey, where it was 21, we had a 'blood border.' Kids were going to New York to drink and then driving home—dying at the borders. So I decided to do some life-saving," says Lautenberg. He met fierce opposition.

Supporters of the "21" law, including NJ senator Frank Lautenberg (far left) and Transportation Secretary Elizabeth Dole (far right), lobby outside of the Capitol in June 1984.

"Restaurant owners and alcohol establishments said I was going to put them out of business. And my two younger kids didn't even want to talk to me. They were in their late teens and said I was killing all their fun," Lautenberg says. "I preferred to kill their 'fun' rather than kill them."

Meanwhile, Hurley was escorting MADD founder Candy Lightner and a CBS News crew through the Senate building.

"Candy and I were going door to door in the Senate to pin them down on their '21' stance. Some senators loved it. Some hated it. One would not let the cameras in for fear that the media was driving the Senate decision," says Hurley, remembering another senator who even flip-flopped on her anti-21 stance once the cameras were rolling.

White House Shift

Ultimately, a shift in the White House's position created the clincher MADD needed.

Despite the official White House stance against a federal 21 drinking bill, President Reagan's Secretary of Transportation Elizabeth Dole really wanted the Administration to support it. "It made such common sense to me," Dole says. Like Senator Lautenberg, she was alarmed by the numbers of young people dying on state "blood borders."

She pressed for an Oval Office meeting with President Reagan. "I wanted to see if I could get the president to come on board with us," she recalls.

Early into that White House meeting, top Reagan advisors Edwin Meese and Michael Deaver reminded the president of his opposition to federal "21" legislation due to states' rights.

Dole says the ensuing dialogue was short and sweet. "The president looked at me and said, 'Well, wait a minute—doesn't this help save kids' lives?'

"I said, 'Yes, Mr. President, it does.'

"'Well, then, I support it,' he said."

The next day, Secretary Dole announced President Reagan's support for the measure during a MADD press conference on the

President Ronald Reagan signs the Uniform Drinking Age Act on July 17, 1984, requiring all fifty states to set twenty-one as the legal drinking age.

Capitol steps. Lautenberg's Senate measure subsequently passed 81-16. And Reagan signed the Uniform Drinking Age Act into law on July 17, 1984.

The Paradox of "21"

Since then, the National Highway Traffic Safety Administration estimates 1,000 lives have been saved each year in alcohol-related traffic crashes—close to 20,000 in the two decades the law has been in effect.

"This does not take into account the number of burns, drownings, sexual assaults, and even suicides and homicides averted by '21' legislation," says MADD's Hamilton.

But there's still work to be done.

"Between alcohol-related automobile crashes, unintentional injuries, and homicides and suicides, my best estimate is that there are 7,000 alcohol-related deaths among people under age 21 annually," says Ralph Hingson, Sc.D., director of the Division of Epidemiology and Prevention Research for the National Institute on Alcohol Abuse and Alcoholism. "There are still a lot of people dying because we're not enforcing these laws."

Hingson also points to what was not known in 1984, but is known now: The brain continues to develop until the early 20s. "Magnetic resonance imaging shows less frontal lobe activity in children who have alcohol dependence," says Hingson, adding that memory, spatial relations and the ability to plan are most affected.

Despite laws setting 21 as the minimum legal drinking age and research showing alcohol damages brain development, the paradox of "21" is this: Underage drinking is America's No. 1 youth drug problem.

Underage drinkers have easy access to alcohol. Drinking laws—if not riddled with loopholes—often are not well enforced. And parents and communities often look the other way.

Loopholes and Law Enforcement

In 1995, the passage of the federal Zero Tolerance Laws gave the 21 drinking age a shot in the arm. Before 1995, it was not against the law in many states for drivers under 21 to drink and drive until their BAC exceeded the legal limit—which was then .08 or .10 percent, depending on the state.

Hingson's research on zero tolerance was critical.

"We looked at eight states that had passed Zero Tolerance Laws and compared them to eight nearby states that had not. We found a 20 percent reduction in single-vehicle, nighttime fatal crashes among 18- to 20-year-olds in states that had Zero Tolerance Laws versus states that did not," he says.

In 1995, Congress passed legislation requiring all states to adopt Zero Tolerance Laws, which make it illegal for anyone under 21 to drive with any measurable amount of alcohol in their system.

Yet other loopholes and legal technicalities still abound. Fourteen states currently do not prohibit underage attempts to purchase alcohol. Fifteen states do not prohibit consumption by underage drinkers. A recent, highly publicized case in Virginia, for example, has shown that the underage consumption law there refers only to "minors," technically making the 18- to 20-year-old group exempt.

Meanwhile, as Senator Lautenberg recently observed while at a rodeo in Montana, enforcement of underage drinking laws is often spotty.

"I noticed a lot of young kids walking around with beer bottles," Lautenberg says.

"So I walked over to a policeman and said, 'Officer, do you know what the legal drinking age is in this country?'

"He said, 'It's 21.'

"I asked him, 'Don't most of these kids look like they're under 21?'

"He said, 'Look mister, I do traffic.'"

Lautenberg swallowed hard that day. "If we saved 20,000 lives just by passing the '21' legislation, maybe we could have saved twice that number with better law enforcement."

Researchers and safety experts agree.

"Most communities could use more active enforcement," says the University of Minnesota's Wagenaar, whose continued research into underage drinking has revealed under-21 buyers often have little trouble buying—and of-age suppliers often go unpunished.

In fact, while Wagenaar says progress has been made since 1994, he estimated then that only five of every 100,000 incidents of underage drinking resulted in a fine, license revocation or license suspension of an alcohol establishment.

"We don't do enforcement of the purchase age anywhere near optimally," Wagenaar says. "Nor do those who sell to underage drinkers think they will get caught. One enforcement check every few years is not enough."

Fix "21"

"Federal 21 legislation was a victory for MADD and a victory for the nation," says MADD's Hamilton. "But so many more young lives will be saved if we fix the remaining flaws in the 21 law."

Federally, MADD recommends the establishment of one lead agency to deal with all underage drinking issues. "Without such a national agency, it makes it hard to see where we are on the scorecard with underage drinking issues," Hingson says.

MADD will also push for additional funding for underage drinking compliance activities, as well as further research into underage drinking.

Finally, MADD will ask Congress to fund and support the development of a national underage drinking media campaign aimed at adults. "It is vital to target adults. Kids get their alcohol from

MADD president Wendy Hamilton speaks to the media in 2005. The organization is urging the government to establish a federal agency to contend with underage drinking.

adults. Adults either sell it to them, give it to them or buy it for them," Hamilton says.

State legislative initiatives will take the battle to the trenches. First, MADD will encourage states to fix the deficiencies in the minimum drinking age law.

Second, MADD will encourage states to bolster existing laws or pass new laws based on measures proven to prevent underage drinking. These include compliance checks, sobriety checkpoints and enforcement of Zero Tolerance and Graduated Licensing Laws.

Public Safety Will Prevail

Looking back to 1984, some things aren't so different today. Society still views underage alcohol use as an acceptable rite of passage. Many still subscribe to the "old-enough-to-vote, old-enough-to-drink" philosophy. And many politicians are still tied to the alcohol industry through campaign donations. That, says Hamilton, creates a hard wall to break down.

But step by step and state by state, she predicts common sense and public safety will prevail.

And in the end, more lives will be saved.

EIGHT

The Legal Drinking Age Should Be Lowered

National Youth Rights Association

In the following FAQ the National Youth Rights Association (NYRA) insists that raising the minimum legal drinking age to twenty-one has not saved twenty thousand lives, as many groups insist. Instead, the authors argue, it unfairly punishes responsible Americans who are mature enough to vote, hold office, and serve in the military. Setting the legal drinking age at twenty-one enforces the common misconception that twenty-one is the "magic" age at which the body and mind are mature enough to handle alcohol, the NYRA contends. In fact, as most medical studies prove, maturity is a gradual process that occurs throughout life. Not only must the legal drinking age be lowered to eighteen, the NYRA maintains, but alcohol should be introduced gradually to teenagers at younger ages in safe environments like the home so that they can learn to drink responsibly. The strict and blind enforcement of the drinking age is misguided and unwise and ultimately hurts more people than it helps, the authors conlude. The National Youth Rights Association is a nonprofit organization dedicated to defending the civil and human rights of young people in the United States.

Editors Note: The following "frequently asked questions" are taken from the National Youth Rights Association's Web site, www.youth rights.org, and examine the reasoning behind lowering the legal drinking age to eighteen.

How many countries have a drinking age of 21?

Only four on the entire planet. Ukraine, South Korea, Malaysia, and the United States. All other countries (out of like 200) have lower drinking ages, and many don't have any drinking age at all.

Did raising the drinking age save 20,000 lives?

No. This is one of the most misguided and over-used statistics circulated by the Youth Prohibitionist movement. The truth is, as researchers Peter Asch and David Levy put it, the "minimum legal drinking age is not a significant—or even a perceptible—factor in the fatality experience of all drivers or of young drivers." In an in-depth and unrefuted study Asch and Levy prove that raising the drinking age merely transferred lost lives from the 18–20 bracket to the 21–24 age group. The problem with the 20,000 lives saved statistic is that it looks only at deaths for people aged 18–20. This is like rating the safety of a car by looking only at the seat belt and ignoring the fact that the car frequently tips over while driving. Raising the drinking age may have reduced deaths [for people aged]18–20 but resulted in more deaths among people 21–24. Raising the drinking age has not done its job, and its time we look at the problem of drinking and driving honestly to find better options for dealing with the problem.

Alcohol and Maturity

People aren't mature enough to handle alcohol till you turn 21. Right?

When you are 18 you are judged mature enough to vote, hold public office, serve on juries, serve in the military, fly airplanes, sign contracts and so on. Why is drinking a beer an act of greater responsibility and maturity than flying an airplane or serving your country at war?

Doesn't your body develop up till the age of 21?

Your body and mind improve all throughout life. A 21 year old is different from an 18 year old, just as a 41 year old is different from a 38 year old. Youth Prohibition activists ignore the fact that maturity is a gradual but uneven process that continues throughout life and is not complete on one's twenty-first birthday. Moreover, they ignore the proven medical fact that the moderate consumption of alcohol is associated with better health and greater longevity than is either abstaining or abusing alcohol. The simplest way to prove this argument is for you to look in your medicine cabinet or go to the drug store. Every single over the counter medication defines an adult dose for ages 12 and up. Not 21, but 12. If the FDA [Food and Drug Administration] can determine that a 12 year old is developed enough to have an equal dose of Tylenol, or Sudafed, or Dramamine, or Zantac 75, then an 18 year old is developed enough to have a glass of wine with dinner.

Sharpnack. © 2003 by Joe Sharpnack. Reproduced by permission.

Young women drink saki at a coming of age ceremony in Tokyo. In Japan a person can legally drink alcohol and vote at age twenty.

Introducing Youth to Alcohol

If 18 year olds obtain alcohol with a 21 drinking age, won't lowering the drinking age to 18 just put alcohol within reach of 15 year olds? Wouldn't this create "low hanging fruit"?

It is true that 18 year olds currently have access to alcohol despite the law. So do most students in high school. In fact—nearly *three-quarters of 8th graders* (71%) say that it is "fairly easy" or "very easy" to get alcohol. If even a solid majority of 13 year olds have easy access to alcohol then clearly a strict no-use Youth Prohibitionist method isn't working and a smarter approach needs to be tried.

NYRA [National Youth Rights Association] argues that a strict no-use policy towards alcohol causes many problems, how will simply lowering the drinking age from 21 to 18 change this?

The National Youth Rights Association doesn't just feel we should lower the age from 21 to 18 and change nothing else. We feel larger change must occur for people under 18 as well. Alcohol must be introduced gradually and at younger ages (12 perhaps) as they do in Europe. Young people must be allowed to get their feet wet through the introduction of alcohol in small amounts in safe environments like the home. Any permanent change to alcohol policy must stress this above all. NYRA feels this period of gradual introduction to alcohol may take a few years, but in no way should it last until 21. If an ending year for introduction is to be named, 18 is far more reasonable.

Safe Consumption of Alcohol

NYRA claims to recognize all the harm alcohol does, if that's true, why do you want to lower the drinking age?

Alcohol can be a very dangerous substance that causes problems for all people. This is as true for a 17 year old as it is for a 39 year old. The danger of alcohol is real and doesn't go away when someone turns 21. If an organization wished to ban alcohol for the entire population equally, then NYRA would have no reason to stand in their way. NYRA is definitely not "pro-alcohol", rather NYRA is "pro-youth" and we find it hypocritical that adults point their finger at youth while holding a beer in the other hand. It is time we recognize, and discuss the truth about alcohol rather than creating a young scapegoat for society to blame their alcohol troubles on. Through education, gradual entry, and a relaxing of strict no-use policy towards youth will make drinking safer for people of all ages.

I'm over 21, do I have a reason to care about the Drinking Age?

Yes. The strict and blind enforcement of the drinking age creates many victims over and under 21. Problems for people over 21 include the hassle of being carded at bars and restaurants, and the problem of social segregation. When going out with friends the drinking age drives a wedge between friends over and under 21. Often they are unable to hang out at the same places. Most troubling is what happens to parents who recognize the inevitability of underage drinking will try to provide safe, supervised places for high school students to have parties. These parents can be punished to ridiculous lengths for their attempts to allow safe drinking. In February 2003 Elsa and George Robinson were sentenced to 8 years in prison for providing alcohol at their son's birthday party. That's right, 8 years. The harsh drinking age ruins more lives than it helps.

Would NYRA be opposed to lowering the legal limit of Blood Alcohol Content(BAC) for drivers?

No. NYRA fiercely and unqualifyingly opposes drinking and driving, it is a dangerous practice that should be stopped. NYRA's one and only concern as an organization is age discrimination, that is why we push to reform drinking age laws. As for other alcohol laws not related to age, it really isn't our concern. If states wanted to lower the BAC to .05 for all drivers it wouldn't matter to us. NYRA supports all non-ageist policies that seek to reduce the deadly practice of drunk driving.

NYRA describes itself as a "youth rights" organization; do you feel youth have a "right" to drink? Isn't this a trivial issue?

Certainly there are more critical issues that affect young people in America than drinking alcohol, but the drinking age is a highly visible example of our current anti-youth culture. The National Youth Rights Association does not feel this is an issue primarily about alcohol; rather it is an issue about equality, honesty, respect, discrimination and freedom. If it were shown that Americans of French descent were more likely to abuse alcohol would it be right to pass a law stopping all French-Americans from drinking? No, that would be discrimination. Americans of all ages, races, genders, and ethnicities deserve equal respect, and they deserve the right to make their own choices in life. Youth deserve nothing less. So whether it is choosing to drink a beer, choosing to stay up late, or choosing the next President, NYRA feels society must respect and honor the choices of young people in an equal, fair and honest way.

NINE

DUI Cases May Be Prosecuted Unfairly

Joseph T. Hallinan

> In the following article excerpt, Joseph T. Hallinan writes that suspected drunk drivers are no longer simply asked to take a breath test. In many states police officers are taking blood samples—in many cases without the driver's consent. At least eight states allow police to use "reasonable force" to get blood samples from drivers suspected of driving under the influence (DUI). However, Hallinan reports, police have used methods to obtain blood that have been challenged in courts as violating civil liberties, including chokeholds, strapping drivers to tables, and applying stun guns. Some suspected drunk drivers are taken to a hospital to have their blood drawn, creating an ethical dilemma for doctors who are honor bound to respect the privacy and needs of their patients. While anti-DUI activists applaud the trend toward an increasing use of blood tests, civil liberties watchdogs consider them a threat to privacy. Joseph T. Hallinan is a staff writer for the *Wall Street Journal*. He has also written for the *Indianapolis Star*, where he won a Pulitzer Prize in 1991.

After police stopped Robert H. Miller for driving erratically [in Brookfield, Wisconsin,] one afternoon in February 2001, they asked for his license and registration.

Then they asked for something else: his blood. Having been convicted of drunk driving once before, Mr. Miller refused to cooperate. So after he was taken to a hospital, five officers pinned him to the floor as a medical technician stuck a needle in his arm. His blood-alcohol level was 0.266%—more than twice the legal limit. Mr. Miller, who declined to comment, challenged the tactic in court but lost. He pleaded no contest, was sentenced to up to 90 days in jail and lost his license for 18 months.

In the past, police routinely asked suspected drunk drivers to blow into devices that extrapolated their blood's alcohol content from their breath. Now, authorities in most states are taking blood, by force if necessary.

"I've really pushed it," says John O'Boyle, district attorney of Pierce County, Wis. Lawyers sometimes successfully challenge breath tests in court or persuade juries to doubt them, but "blood tests tend to be pretty bulletproof," Mr. O'Boyle says. Moreover, it's impossible to force a breath test on someone, but taking blood requires no cooperation. "If we have to literally strap you down if you refuse, that's what can happen to you," says Lt. Tony Almaraz, a Nevada Highway Patrol spokesman.

Advocates say blood tests, once seldom used, now are a powerful weapon against drunk driving. But the tests raise two nettlesome questions: How much force should police be able to use in extracting blood from uncooperative suspects? And should medical professionals, who are honor-bound to obey patients' treatment wishes and protect their privacy, be compelled to do otherwise?

Blood Tests Today

For half a century, breath tests have been the standard in the U.S. and remain in wide use. But as penalties for driving under the influence increased, many suspects started refusing to submit, figuring the penalty for declining—often a one-year license suspension—beats a DUI [driving under the influence] conviction.

The National Highway Traffic Safety Administration found in a 1991 survey of 40 states that 19% of drivers arrested for DUI

A drunk driver in Costa Mesa, California, is handcuffed and led to a squad car after failing both a breathalyzer and blood test.

refused to be tested. More recent figures suggest that problem persists, with nearly 8,900 Massachusetts drivers, 11,900 Missouri drivers and 23,500 Florida drivers declining tests in 2001, officials in those states say.

Frustrated by the increasing savvy of drunks and defense attorneys, at least eight states—Alaska, Arizona, Iowa, Florida, Indiana, Michigan, Nevada and Texas—have in recent years enacted statutes specifically permitting police to use reasonable force to obtain blood samples in DUI cases.

Laws in at least seven other states allow police to take blood without the driver's consent, without explicitly authorizing force. In most other states, court rulings have authorized reasonable force to obtain blood. Many such rulings cite a little-known fact about driving laws in the U.S.: All motorists are considered to have consented to a search of their blood, breath or urine. Such "implied consent" laws were introduced in New York in 1953, and today all 50 states and the District of Columbia have them.

The circumstances under which blood can be taken vary. In some states, blood can be taken only from repeat offenders or in

Many states allow police to take blood samples from suspected drunk drivers without their consent. Several other states allow police to use reasonable force to obtain a sample.

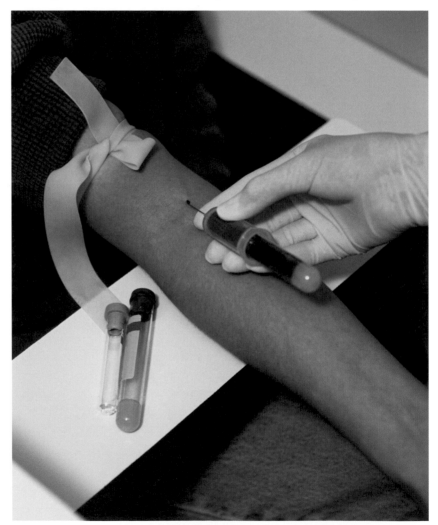

cases where people are killed or injured in crashes. Some allow exceptions for members of religious groups that oppose certain medical treatments and for those with health conditions that make blood draws dangerous, such as hemophiliacs. Warrants usually aren't required because alcohol dissipates from the bloodstream, leaving police little time to seek one—an "exigent circumstance" long allowed by courts as an exception to Fourth Amendment warrant requirements.

An Increase in Blood Tests

No national statistics exist, but in Wisconsin the number of blood samples taken from DUI suspects has doubled since 1995, to 21,418 in 2003. State officials didn't track how many were legally intoxicated, but they say that in 92% of the 38,214 DUI cases handled in 2002, the drivers were convicted.

Alarmed by what they see as diminished police vigilance, anti-DUI activists praise the trend toward increased reliance on blood evidence. As the number of licensed drivers in the U.S. climbed, DUI arrests fell to about 1.5 million in 2002 from a 1990 peak of 1.8 million, and the estimated number of alcohol-related traffic deaths edged up slightly, to 17,419 in 2002. Drunk driving remains the second-most-common crime in the U.S. behind drug offenses.

Critics of the practice see a threat to privacy and civil liberties, with judges in Rhode Island, New Jersey and Wisconsin barring, limiting or questioning the practice in recent years. In Pennsylvania, the state police say they don't take blood if a driver refuses, but might if the driver is unconscious.

Problems with Blood Tests

The ways in which blood is drawn vary considerably. Under one common scenario, drivers are stopped by police and asked to perform a field sobriety test. If they fail this, they are taken to a medical facility, such as a hospital, and blood is drawn there.

Some physicians are alarmed when doctors or those working for them draw blood for police without consent. The doctors argue that the Hippocratic Oath requires them to put patients' needs and desires first and to respect their privacy and decisions to decline medical procedures. The American College of Emergency Physicians said in 1998 that it opposes requiring or permitting doctors to give blood-test results to police "because such reporting fundamentally conflicts with the appropriate role of physicians in the physician-patient relationship."

"For me to draw blood from a patient who is refusing to have his blood drawn, unless I have compelling medical reasons for that blood sample, I'm committing assault and battery, and I'm not going to do it," says Dr. Phil Brewer, president of the Connecticut College of Emergency Physicians and a fellow at the National Highway Traffic Safety Administration.

Dr. Brewer says some doctors fear that reporting alcohol levels to the police might violate the Health Insurance Portability and Accountability Act, which makes the unauthorized disclosure of patients' records a crime. "Who's willing to take that risk?" he asks. "I don't want to be the test case." . . .

Blood Tests and the Law

The U.S. Supreme Court last addressed taking blood against a driver's wishes in a 1966 case, *Schmerber v. California*. The defendant crashed his car into a tree after drinking at a tavern and a bowling alley. Injured, he was taken to the hospital. Police thought he looked drunk and directed a doctor to obtain a blood sample over the man's objection. He didn't physically resist, but challenged the action in an appeal of his DUI conviction. The Supreme Court ruled, 5-4, that the incident didn't violate his Fifth Amendment right against compelled self-incrimination or his Fourth Amendment right against unreasonable searches and seizures.

The majority stressed, however, that the decision was narrow, based on the "reasonable manner" in which the blood was obtained—"by a physician in a hospital environment." The majority warned that "serious questions . . . would arise" if the blood were extracted "in other than a medical environment—for example, if it were administered by police in the privacy of the station-

In 1966 the Supreme Court ruled that taking blood from drivers without consent did not violate their right against self-incrimination or unreasonable search and seizure.

house" because allowing that might "invite an unjustified element of personal risk of infection and pain." It added that "more substantial intrusions, or intrusions under other conditions" might not pass muster.

These days, though, blood often is obtained under much different circumstances and sometimes via more forceful means.

State and federal courts have countenanced a range of police conduct in obtaining blood, from putting a chokehold on the carotid artery of a suspected drunk in California to shooting one in the arm with a stun-gun in Delaware.

And blood often is extracted in police lockups and jailhouses—just the sort of environment the Supreme Court said might be constitutionally troublesome.

Testimony in a federal suit last year [2003] shows that authorities in Las Vegas regularly obtain blood samples in the Clark County Detention Center. The suit involved a 1998 incident. Police found Terry Jones, then 33, asleep at the wheel of a parked car, an open Budweiser between his thighs. He was arrested, taken to the jail and ordered to submit to a blood test. Mr. Jones, who had two prior DUI convictions, put up a furious fight.

Stopped by police on suspicion of drunk driving in December 2000, actress Shannen Doherty was given a nonconsensual blood test. She was arrested with a BAC of .13.

Guard Daniel Kresky testified that physical resistance to blood draws was a nightly event. Guards would use "whatever force is necessary," he testified, typically handcuffing defendants' arms behind their back, bending them over an examination table in the jail nurse's office and holding them down. Sometimes, drivers were held on the floor. "We always got our blood," he testified.

Mr. Jones, 270 pounds, tossed several officers off his back with a buck of his head. Two officers testified that another stood on and kicked Mr. Jones's head; that officer denied the charge. Suddenly, Mr. Jones went limp. The coroner ruled that Mr. Jones died of acute cardiac arrhythmia, a heart-rhythm disturbance. But a second autopsy, performed by a retired deputy medical examiner at the request of Mr. Jones's widow, found that his head had been beaten and his left eye crushed. "Had it not been for that trauma, he probably wouldn't have died," that doctor testified.

Last March [2003], a jury ruled that police and jail officials weren't responsible. Paul Martin, the jail's chief, says it now uses a specially-made chair with Velcro straps to restrain drivers brought in for forced blood draws.

Questioning Forced Blood Draws

Encounters over drivers' blood are beginning to give some judges second thoughts.

In a Rhode Island case, police in 1997 arrested a woman on suspicion of DUI after a car she was driving struck and killed a motorcyclist. She submitted to a breath test, which found only minimal alcohol, but she refused to give blood, so the police got a warrant. Her blood tested positive for marijuana and cocaine.

In pretrial litigation, the state Supreme Court ruled in 2000 that taking her blood without consent violated a provision in the state's implied-consent law, which says that if a driver refuses to submit to a test, "none shall be given." The court said the provision was meant to "prevent a violent confrontation between an arresting officer and a suspect unwilling to submit." (The defendant later pleaded no contest to DUI resulting in death.) Some state lawmakers advocated changing the law to allow force, but the Legislature hasn't done so.

A year later, the New Jersey Supreme Court ruled that police in Edgewater went too far when they pinned a screaming, struggling suspected drunk driver to a hospital table, strapped down his legs and left arm and held him while a nurse drew eight vials of blood, which indicated that he was drunk. The court didn't bar the future use of force outright but said that under the circumstances the police used "unreasonable force." Barred from using blood evidence, prosecutors retried the man, who was convicted based on police testimony that he seemed drunk.

In Wisconsin, state Court of Appeals Judge Charles Schudson says in an interview that the state's blood-drawing practices come "painfully, painfully close to a violation of civil liberties." An outspoken critic of DUI laws he deems too lax, Judge Schudson voted to uphold the use of force to obtain blood but only because he concluded that Wisconsin legal precedent required that he do so. In a Court of Appeals opinion written in 2002, he took the unusual step of asking the state Supreme Court to reverse its previous decisions supporting forced blood draws. So far, it has not done so.

TEN

Forced Blood Draws in DUI Cases Are Legal

Bruce Nelson and Tera Ames

In the following article Bruce Nelson and Tera Ames explain that the U.S. Supreme Court has ruled that it is legal for police to use reasonable force to obtain a blood sample from a suspected drunken driver. Reasonable force is defined as the force necessary to overcome the resistance of the suspected offender, which gives police great latitude. In addition, in some circumstances police may legally use stun guns and place suspected offenders in chokeholds in order to obtain a blood sample. However, the authors note, police only resort to force after a suspect refuses to provide a blood sample. Furthermore, Nelson and Ames states, several courts have ruled that suspects do not have the right to demand to take an alternative blood alcohol concentration test, such as a breath or urine test. The legal system has clearly established the principle that a suspected drunk driver must provide a blood sample when asked to do so. Bruce Nelson and Tera Ames are deputy district attorneys with the vehicular crimes unit of the Clark County District Attorney's office in Nevada.

Bruce Nelson and Tera Ames, "Forced Blood Draws in DUI Cases Is Legal," *Communiqué: The Official Publication of the Clark County Bar*, February 2003.

The Supreme Court has ruled that the use of reasonable force to perform blood tests on suspected drunk drivers is constitutional.

A person who drives a vehicle in Nevada has given their consent to providing a sample of their blood, breath, urine or other bodily fluid when lawfully requested to do so by a police officer.[1]

So what happens when a person decides to revoke their consent and refuse to provide a sample? Until 1995, such a person suffered two sanctions: the fact finder could infer guilt based on their refusal and their driver's license was revoked for one year. However, in 1995, the Nevada Legislature amended [the law] . . . to provide, in pertinent part:

If a person to be tested fails to submit to a required test as directed by a police officer pursuant to this section and the officer has reasonable grounds to believe that the person to

1. according to Nevada law, NRS 484.383

be tested was: (a) Driving . . . a vehicle while under the influence of intoxicating liquor or a controlled substance; . . . the officer may direct that reasonable force be used to the extent necessary to obtain samples of blood from the person to be tested. . . .

A History of the Law of Forcible Blood Draws

In *Rochin v. California*, (1952), the Supreme Court found that the Due Process Clause was violated when the police used a stomach pump to obtain evidence that the defendant had swallowed. Five years later in *Breinthaupt v. Abram*, (1957), the Supreme Court found that a blood sample obtained from an unconscious DUI [driving under the influence] suspect did not violate the Due Process Clause.

The first Supreme Court case to specifically address the issue of a forced blood draw from a conscious defendant was *Schmerber v. California*, (1966). Schmerber had been involved in an auto accident and was at the local hospital. Suspecting that Schmerber might be under the influence of alcohol, the police asked Schmerber to provide a blood sample. Although Schmerber refused based on advice of counsel, his blood was taken without his consent. Schmerber offered no physical resistance to the taking of his blood.

The Court, relying on *Breinthaupt*, found that a routine blood draw by a medical technician did not violate the Due Process Clause. The Court did caution that the result could be different if the police initiated violence to obtain a blood sample, refused a reasonable request to undergo another form of testing or used unreasonable force to obtain a blood sample. The Court found that exigent circumstances justified the warrantless drawing of Schmerber's blood because his blood alcohol level would dissipate if his blood was not immediately collected. The Court also found that providing a blood sample was non-testimonial in nature and was therefore not subject to the privilege against self incrimination.

Schmerber was followed by *South Dakota v. Neville*, (1983). Neville refused to take a blood test and his refusal was introduced against him at trial as an admission of guilt. The Court upheld the introduction of his refusal.

Based on the findings in *Schmerber* and *Neville*, there is little doubt that the police may use force to obtain a blood sample from a suspected drunk driver. . . .

Both the U.S. Supreme Court and, apparently, the Nevada Supreme Court, permit the forcible drawing of blood from a suspected drunk driver. The only restrictions on the forcible blood draw are that the draw must be done in a medically acceptable manner and only reasonable force be used to obtain the blood sample. Nevada law provides that the blood test will be given in a medically acceptable manner because the test may only be given by a limited number of trained medical personnel. However, [current Nevada law] does not define the phrase "reasonable force be used to the extent necessary to obtain samples of blood from the person to be tested." To determine what type of force may be used to obtain a blood sample one must look to other states.

A Definition of Reasonable Force

The reasonable force necessary to obtain a blood sample has been addressed by several states. In a nutshell, "reasonable force" has been defined as the force necessary to overcome the resistance of the defendant to the blood draw. Under this definition, the police have been given great latitude. For example, in *McCann v. State*, (1991), the police used a stun gun to immobilize a resisting defendant so that a blood sample could be obtained. In *Carleton v. Superior Court*, (1985), one officer applied a choke hold on Carleton while five other officers held him down for the blood draw. In a similar vein, *State v. Lanier*, (1990), and *State v. Myers*, (1990), permitted multiple officers to immobilize a combative defendant.

Reasonable force to obtain a blood sample is defined by, and determined by, the amount of resistance given by a defendant. The first *Schmerber* caution, police-initiated violence, should never

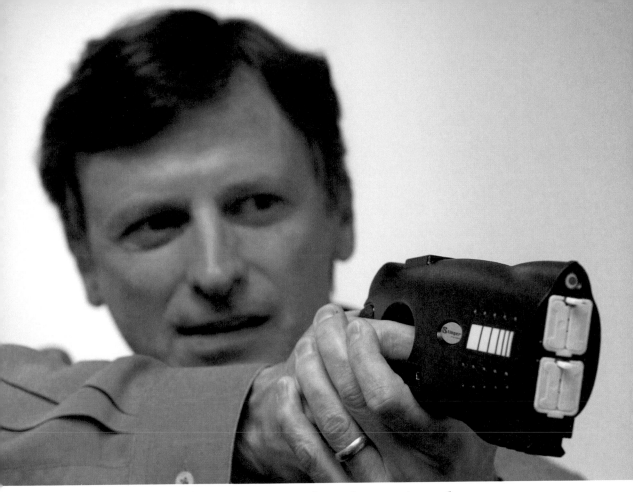

Courts have ruled that stun guns, such as the one pictured here, can be used to immobilize suspected drunk drivers in order to take a blood sample.

occur in the context of a blood draw. As a practical matter, the police have no incentive to initiate violence to obtain a blood sample. Realistically, the police will offer a suspect the option of a blood draw. Only after the suspect refuses to give a blood sample would the police resort to force to obtain the blood sample. The second caution, unreasonable force, occasionally has occurred, but, as noted, courts give the police wide latitude in the amount of force that may be used to compel a resistant defendant to give a blood sample.

Finally, the third *Schmerber* factor, unreasonably refusing an alternative test, has not received much support in post-*Schmerber* decisions. Several courts have addressed the question of whether a defendant's request to take an alternative test must be respected. The nearly uniform answer has been "no." In *Kostyk v. Commonwealth*, (1990), the police told Kostyk that he had to take a blood test. Kostyk later appealed the suspension of his license for refusing to take the blood test on the ground that the police should not have unfettered discretion in selecting the type of test that a defendant must take. The *Kostyk* Court, citing *Schmerber*, found that a compulsory blood test was constitutional and that the right to refuse a test is a matter of legislative grace. Nevada law allows a defendant to have his own chemical test performed but only after he has taken the State's test.

Reasonable Force Defined in Other Cases

One court has utilized the "alternative test" factor to impose civil liability against the police for refusing to allow an alternative test.

Varvel. © 2005 by Creators Syndicate. Reproduced by permission.

In *Nelson v. City of Irvine*, (1998), the court permitted a class action suit against the police based on an alternative test theory. The class members argued that California law allowed an arrestee the choice of a blood, breath or urine test and that the police were compelling arrestees to take blood tests. Interestingly, the court found that the police did not violate the Fourth Amendment when they failed to advise an arrestee of the choice of tests; a violation only occurred when the arrestee requested a breath or urine test and the police refused to honor that request. The *Nelson* court stopped short of holding that state law must give a defendant a choice of tests but, because California law offered such a choice, the arrestee's request for an alternative test must be permitted.

Nelson's failure to hold that State law must grant a choice of tests to a defendant limits its utility to a defendant who wishes to argue that his "right" to choose an alternative test was violated. Several post-*Nelson* decisions have distinguished *Nelson* on the ground that, while California law grants a choice of tests to an arrestee, their state laws permit the officer to choose the type of test to be given. *State v. Clary*, (2000) and *In Re Halen*, (2002). Nevada law mandates a blood test for a DUI felony or where the officer reasonably believes the arrestee has a prior conviction within seven years; a defendant with no prior convictions has a choice of a blood or breath test.

The principle that a suspected drunk driver must provide a blood sample for testing when lawfully requested to do so is firmly established in the law. Likewise, the principle that the police may use reasonable force to obtain a blood sample from a resisting arrestee is also firmly established . . . , a defendant has no legal basis to challenge the forcible extraction of his blood for alcohol testing. A defendant's blood alcohol level is an effective tool in determining his guilt or innocence to the charge of driving under the influence. Decisions by various courts have ensured that this tool will be available to both the State and the defendant.

ELEVEN

Repeat Drunk Drivers Should Be Severely Punished

National Hardcore Drunk Driver Project

In the following selection, the National Hardcore Drunk Driver Project defines hardcore drunk drivers as those who drive with a blood alcohol concentration (BAC) of 0.15 or above, who do so repeatedly, and who are highly resistant to changing their behavior despite previous legal sanctions, treatment, or education. Although hardcore drunk drivers make up only 1 percent of all drivers on weekend nights, the project notes, they are involved in nearly half of all fatal crashes during this time. The author insists that drivers with high BACs deserve stiffer punishment than those with lower BACs because they are more likely to be dangerous on the road. A graduated system of sanctions, in which more severe penalties are given to repeat drivers or those with a high BAC, penalizes drunk drivers more fairly, the project concludes. In addition, promising research shows that the graduated system may ultimately curb hardcore drunk drivers. The National Hardcore Drunk Driver Project was created by the Century Council, a national, not-for-profit organization, to assist in reducing the number of fatalities, injuries, and damage caused by chronic drunk drivers.

In 2001, 17,448 people were killed in alcohol-related traffic crashes and 275,000 were injured in the United States. That represents an average of one alcohol-related fatality every 30 minutes and one person injured approximately every two minutes. In addition to injuries and the loss of lives, drunk driving carries a huge economic price tag.

While comprising a relatively small proportion of drivers, the impact of hardcore drunk drivers in human and monetary costs far exceeds their actual numbers. For example:

- It is estimated that while drivers with BACs [blood alcohol concentration] in excess of .15 are only 1 percent of all drivers on weekend nights, they are involved in nearly 50 percent of all fatal crashes at that time.

A rescue worker uses the jaws of life to remove the body of an auto accident victim.

- About one-third of all drivers arrested for DWI [driving while intoxicated] are repeat offenders and over half have a BAC over .15.
- In the United States in 2001, 22 percent of all drivers killed in motor vehicle crashes and 57 percent of all drinking drivers in an alcohol-related fatal crash had BAC levels of .15 or greater.
- Drivers with a BAC of .15 or above are 385 times more likely to be involved in a single vehicle fatal crash than the average non-drinking driver.

A strong relationship exists between a high BAC and the likelihood of having a previous DWI conviction. The 2001 Fatality Analysis Reporting System (FARS) data show that previous DWI convictions increase in direct correlation with increases in BAC in subsequent arrests.

States with "High BAC" Laws

"High BAC" laws allow the courts to impose harsher punishments on those convicted of driving with a blood alcohol concentration of 0.15, nearly twice the legal limit.

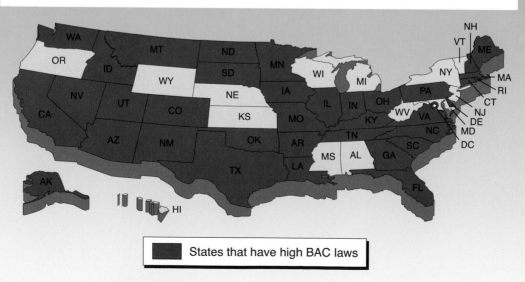

States that have high BAC laws

Source: Mothers Against Drunk Driving, www.madd.org.

For example, only 1.4 percent of non-drinking drivers involved in a fatal crash had a prior DWI conviction compared to 18.5 percent of those with BACs of .15 to .19. This percentage increases to 30.5 percent for those with a BAC of .20 or above. FARS estimates also indicate 77 percent of fatally injured drinking drivers with a BAC above .10 had a prior DWI conviction, while 58 percent of fatally injured drinking drivers with previous DWIs had BACs of .15 and over.

At any BAC level, the risk of apprehension for drunk driving is extremely low, depending on the level of enforcement and the method of calculation. Estimates range from about one arrest in 50 trips to one arrest in 100 trips. Consequently, many hardcore drunk drivers go undetected and aren't reflected in any statistics. Compounding the problem is that hardcore drunk drivers are highly resistant to changing their behavior. That resistance is often characterized by repeat DWI convictions despite previous sanctions, education or treatment. Approximately 30 percent of all drinking drivers arrested for DWI have been caught in the past by the police and sanctioned by judicial and administrative agencies. . . .

Sanctioning Hardcore Drunk Drivers: A Graduated System

The most common means of identifying and punishing hardcore offenders is by determining repeat offenses. Multiple convictions with increasing sanctions and rehabilitation requirements are strong indicators of hardcore behavior—repeatedly driving drunk and being highly resistant to change. The vast majority of states treat repeat drunk driving more severely and have statutory provisions for graduated penalties based on number of offenses. States differ, however, as to how long they maintain records on repeat offenses and the time frame applicable to be considered a repeat offender.

Almost all states have graduated penalties based upon prior convictions, and 31 states, plus Washington, D.C., and American Samoa, have graduated penalty systems based on blood alcohol concentration (BAC) at the time of arrest. The severity of the penalty increases with

BAC, and sanctions are the most severe for multiple offenders. The system recognizes that drivers with high BACs—most often defined as .15 and above—warrant stiffer sanctions because they are more dangerous on the highway and may also be more likely to repeat the behavior. Plus, many treatment professionals associate a high BAC at arrest with a higher likelihood of alcohol abuse. The primary objective of strong sanctions for high BAC offenders is to reduce recidivism by increasing the certainty and severity of punishment and by reducing loopholes in the system.

States' high BAC sanctioning systems vary greatly, with enhanced sanctions including:

- longer or more intensive alcohol education or treatment;
- limitations on plea reductions or deferred judgments;
- driver-based punitive sanctions such as license suspensions;
- vehicle-based punitive sanctions such as ignition interlocks; and
- courts' consideration of a high BAC in sentencing as an aggravating or special factor.

In a few states, there are no graduated penalties based on BAC, but first offenders with a high BAC must have an alcohol assessment or they can be precluded from programs oriented to less dangerous offenders. Research suggests an effective policy is to treat first-time offenders with extremely high BACs (.20 or higher) as hardcore offenders relative to sanctions, fines, treatment and rehabilitation. Two reasons are cited for this: first, the risk of a crash is much greater at high BACs; and second, driving with an extremely high BAC may indicate the driver has developed a high alcohol tolerance, which also may be an indication of an alcohol problem. Additionally, in a number of states, a high BAC decreases the likelihood of a favorable plea bargain or is taken into account by the judge at sentencing.

Where Are Graduated BAC Systems Used?

According to the National Hardcore Drunk Driver Project Survey, 31 states and Washington, D.C., and American Samoa had grad-

Most states impose severely harsh penalties on drunk drivers with blood alcohol concentrations of .15 and higher, well above the legal limit of .08.

uated BAC systems and enhanced sanctions for high BAC offenders. According to [A.T.] McCartt's 2001 study, most states with graduated systems report few problems with implementing high BAC sanctions and believe the sanctions have had a positive impact on the state's DUI system.

In Colorado, high BAC offenders at .15 and above are subject to a fine of $500–$1,500 and a mandatory incarceration of 90 days for first and subsequent offenses. The mandatory incarceration time can be reduced to 10 days if the offender participates in an alcohol education/treatment program.

In Connecticut, convicted offenders with BAC levels of .16 or above are subject to increased administrative licensing actions. On a first offense, the license is suspended for 120 days. On a second offense, it is suspended for 10 months and on a third offense, the license is suspended for two years and six months.

In Minnesota, first-time offenders with a high BAC level of .20 and above at the time of arrest or within two hours of the time of the offense are charged with third-degree drunk driving (a gross misdemeanor), and the driver's license and license plates are impounded administratively upon arrest. For second offenders at .20 BAC and above, the charge is second-degree drunk driving (a gross misdemeanor), the driver's license and license plates are impounded administratively, and the vehicle is forfeited upon arrest. Additionally, license suspension/revocation periods are doubled for those offenders charged with driving at .20 BAC and above.

In American Samoa, the offenders' BAC is multiplied by a certain constant figure to determine the monetary fines. Offenders with higher BACs are required to pay increased fines.

How Effective Are BAC Graduated Systems?

According to a recent study [by A. McCartt and V. Shabanova] of Minnesota's high BAC law, "high BAC sanctioning systems are viewed as one of the few promising approaches for reducing recidivism among 'hardcore' impaired drivers." Minnesota's high-BAC law appears to have successfully increased the severity of case dispositions for high-BAC offenders, and evidence suggests an initial reduction in recidivism.

Though a specific reduction in recidivism cannot be attributed directly to a tiered BAC system, experts in the field say the graduated penalty system results in increased efficiency and effectiveness in identifying and processing drunk drivers. In 1999, the National Hardcore Drunk Driver Project called for graduated penalties of aggravated DWI and hardcore DWI for high BAC offenders and high BAC repeat offenders, respectively. In its proposal for a model program to reduce hardcore drunk driving, the National Transportation Safety Board (NTSB) recommends all states adopt legislation defining a high blood alcohol concentration (.15 percent or greater) as an "aggravated" DWI offense requiring strong intervention similar to that ordinarily prescribed for repeat DWI offenders.

TWELVE

The Future of DUI Laws

Lawrence Taylor

Lawrence Taylor is a defense attorney who specializes in driving under the influence (DUI) cases. He publishes the online blog www.duiblog.com. In the following blog entry, he writes that the future of DUI laws is bleak. Anti–drunk driving groups will continue to champion laws that increasingly erode the civil liberties of Americans, he predicts, allowing the use of unreliable devices such as cheap breathalyzers as well as the complete loss of trial by jury. In addition, Taylor continues, laws will increasingly focus on facilitating arrests of people with even a trace of alcohol in their blood rather than focusing on drunk drivers who pose a true danger on the road. The legal blood alcohol concentration (BAC) limit will fall from .08 to .05, he suggests, and eventually "zero tolerance" laws will be applied to drivers of all ages. Ultimately, innocent drivers will fall victim to traps set by a corrupt, national DUI system powered by anti-alcohol zealots, Taylor concludes.

I gave a lecture to a national organization of attorneys . . . in which I was asked, among other things, to anticipate the future course of DUI [driving under the influence] laws in the United States. Bearing in mind the words of [American politician] Adlai Stevenson ("We can chart our future clearly and wisely only when we know the path which has led to the present"), I predicted the following. . . .

DUI Laws

The Past: The original laws simply outlawed driving while impaired. With the arrival of primitive breathalyzers, and the counsel of the American Medical Association, impairment was presumed with a blood-alcohol concentration (BAC) of .15%.

A group of high school students watches a skit designed to illustrate the severe consequences of drinking and driving during their upcoming prom night.

Over the years this was dropped to .10%, then .08%, and finally the laws were added making the BAC—not impairment—the offense. There are now bills before state legislatures to drop it to .05%. So-called "zero tolerance" made it a crime for drivers under 21 to have even .01% BAC.

The Trend: From focusing on actual impairment, to facilitating arrests and convictions by focusing on artificial BAC levels—and, finally, to the mere *presence* of alcohol. The emphasis has shifted from addressing the danger (impaired drivers) to facilitating arrests and convictions.

The Future: The "zero tolerance" laws will be applied to drivers of all ages. Criminal liability will be expanded to include *attempted* drunk driving (regardless of lack of specific intent), as well as vicarious liability: accomplices ("aiding and abetting"), conspiracy and so-called "Dram Shop Act" liability (providing a drink to someone who may drive).

A Broader Range of Evidence Will Be Accepted

The Past: Originally, the arresting officer gave his opinion of impairment based upon his observations of driving and symptoms, as well as field sobriety tests. The emphasis shifted to increasingly sophisticated breathalyzers and to blood tests administered by nurses or technicians. However, portable and handheld breath testing devices have more recently been used at the scene to determine probable cause to arrest; the later test on a more sophisticated breathalyzer at the station continues to be used as evidence in court. Some courts are beginning to accept the portable units into evidence.

The Trend: An increasing emphasis on money and expediency rather than accuracy and reliability.

The Future: Evidentiary breathalyzers will be replaced with simpler, cheaper (and less accurate) handheld units at the scene of arrest. Blood samples will be obtained by the officer with his syringe at the scene. Saliva tests may gain acceptance.

The Past: There has been a parade of adverse Supreme Court decisions and a steady erosion of constitutional rights in drunk driving cases—what I have called "The DUI Exception to the

States with License Revocation Laws

Administrative license revocation laws (also called administration license suspension) require that revocation or suspension of the driver's license of people who fail or refuse to take a test of their blood alcohol concentrations (BAC).

States that have license revocation laws

Source: Mothers Against Drunk Driving, www.madd.org.

Constitution". These have included approval of sobriety roadblocks (*Sitz v. Michigan*); double jeopardy (immediate license suspensions followed by criminal prosecutions); right to counsel; self-incrimination (*Neville v. South Dakota*); presumptions of innocence (if .08%, then presumed under the influence; if test taken within 3 hours of driving, BAC presumed to be same as when driving); confrontation; jury trial (*Blanton v. North Las Vegas*); etc.

The Trend: From the protection of the citizen from police violations, to the protection of the police from legal interference.

The Future: Increasing loss of constitutional protection—notably, the complete loss of the right to a jury trial. With the clear focus on cost and expediency, DUI cases will be handled in an administrative setting as license suspensions currently are: the two procedures will simply be consolidated, although criminal penalties will remain. There may be no judge, but only an administrative hearing officer.

A Stronger Federal Role

The Past: DUI laws have always been a state-prescribed crime. With the prompting of special interest groups like MADD (Mothers Against Drunk Driving) and the desire of politicians to curry favor with voters, this has gradually changed. Using a "carrot and stick" approach with highway funds, the federal government has forced states to change their laws and penalties in such ways as: "per se" laws; .08% BAC; "zero tolerance" for drivers under 21; automatic license suspensions; standardized field sobriety tests; federally approved lists of breath testing machines.

The Trend: The federalizing of a traditionally state offense.

The Future: With the use of the Constitution's Commerce Clause, DUI laws and penalties will become "federalized". However, without the ability (or inclination) to arrest and prosecute these crimes in the federal courts, the states will be left to continue processing them in their own courts or administrative hearings.

The New Prohibition

The Past: The Eighteenth Amendment to the Constitution was primarily a woman's movement that ended as a failed experiment. Since then . . . the BAC levels for DUI have steadily dropped from .15% to .08%, and there are efforts to reduce it further. Drivers under 21 already face .01%—alcohol prohibition as to driving.

The Trend: In 1999, MADD (primarily a woman's movement) formally changed its mission statement from drunk driving to include "the problem of underage drinking" (not underage drinking *and* driving). The "problem" of drinking at all is on the horizon.

The Future: The movement will again fail, this time without obtaining a constitutional amendment. This country needs alcohol and drugs too much.

What You Should Know About Drunk Driving

Facts About Drunk Diving:

- According to the National Highway Traffic Safety Administration, 16,694 people were killed in alcohol-related traffic accidents in 2004. This number is down from 17,105 in 2003, a 2 percent decline.
- Thirty-nine percent of automobile fatalities occur in alcohol-related crashes.
- About 1.5 million drivers were arrested for driving under the influence of alcohol or narcotics in 2002.

Facts About Drunk Driving Laws:

- Blood alcohol concentration is a measure of the amount of alcohol in a person's blood. To reach a .08 BAC level, a man weighing 170 pounds would need to consume about four drinks in one hour on an empty stomach. A woman weighing 137 pounds would need to consume about three drinks in one hour on an empty stomach.
- When a person has a BAC of .08, the following driving functions are impaired:
  - judging distance and speed
  - steering
  - visual tracking
  - concentration
  - braking
  - staying in driving lanes
- A driver with a BAC of .08 is eleven times as likely to be in a fatal accident as a driver who has not been drinking alcohol.
- All fifty states and the District of Columbia have .08 BAC laws, meaning it is illegal to drive with a blood alcohol level at or above .08.

- A 2001 study by the Center for Disease Control and Prevention found that .08 BAC laws led to a 13.7 decrease in the number of drunk drivers involved in fatal automobile accidents.
- All states and the District of Columbia have "zero tolerance" laws, which make it illegal for anyone under the age of twenty-one to drive with a BAC of .02 or higher.
- Thirty-seven states have "high BAC" laws, which call for increased punishments for BACs higher than .15. These punishments include:
  - one-year revocation of driver's license
  - vehicle impoundment
  - incarceration
  - house arrest
  - fines
  - payment of restitution to victims
  - substance abuse assessment and treatment
- Fifty-eight percent of alcohol-related fatalities involve someone with a BAC of .15 or higher.
- Aministrative license revocation laws, also called administration license suspension, call for the revocation or suspension of a driver's license for failure to pass or refusal to take a BAC test. Forty-two states and the District of Columbia have such laws.
- Forty-one states have laws that allow the use of sobriety checkpoints to stop cars and screen out drunk drivers.
- Ignition interlock systems are devices that are attached to the steering wheel of cars to prevent people who have been drinking alcohol from driving. The driver must breathe into the device, which then tests the driver's breath for alcohol. If alcohol is detected, the car will not start. Ignition interlock systems are installed on the cars of repeat drunk drivers. Forty-five states employ such systems.
- Forty-seven states require a mandatory jail sentence for drivers who are convicted of their second driving under the influence (DUI) offense.
- Twenty-seven states have laws that allow the cars of repeat drunk drivers to be impounded for a predetermined time period.
- For a complete state-by-state breakdown of drunk-driving laws, visit MADD.org.

What You Should Do About Drunk Driving

Know the Law

In order to know what to do about drunk driving, the first thing you need to do is learn the laws. It is perfectly legal for people over the age of twenty-one to drink alcohol. However, all states have laws against driving under the influence of alcohol. These are known as DUI laws. Specifically, every state in America forbids driving with a blood alcohol concentration (BAC) of .08 or higher. In order to have a .08 BAC level, a man weighing 170 pounds wound need to consume about four drinks in one hour. A woman weighing 137 pounds would need to consume about three drinks in an hour.

This legal limit is based on the theory that alcohol impairs certain functions that are necessary for safe driving. For example, alcohol reduces a person's ability to concentrate, to steer straight, and to judge distances and speeds. For these reasons, people who are intoxicated by alcohol run a much higher risk of crashing than people who are sober. These crashes often result in injuries, deaths, and large economic and social costs.

Although it is illegal in the United States for people under twenty-one to drink alcohol, many do so anyway. And unfortunately, many of these young people end up behind the wheel of a car—often with tragic consequences. Because of the great risk associated with teen drunk driving, every state in the nation has a "zero tolerance" law on the books. These laws make it illegal for anyone under twenty-one to drive with a BAC of .02 or higher (some states forbid a BAC higher than .00).

Specific penalties for driving under the influence vary from state to state, but they generally include fines, community service, suspension or revocation of driving privileges, vehicle impoundment, mandatory assessment and treatment for alcohol problems, and even jail time. The punishments become more severe if you are convicted of a second, third, or subsequent offense.

Plan Ahead

Because of the risks associated with drunk driving, you should not drive if you have been drinking, nor should you ride in a car driven by someone who has been drinking. This advice may prove simpler in theory than in practice. After all, alcohol affects a person's judgment. If you have been drinking, you may be able to convince yourself that you (or your driver) are sober enough to drive even if you are not. For that reason, plan ahead if you are going out with friends. If you are under twenty-one, of course, it is illegal to drink. Regardless of whether you drink, assign a designated driver to be a nondrinker for the evening.

If you find yourself in a situation in which you need a ride and the person available to drive has been drinking, do not get in the car. This may take some courage, especially if you are trying to gain the acceptance of the group you are with. However, it is better to risk losing a few friends than to risk losing your life in a drunk-driving accident. Also, try to prevent your friends or other acquaintances from driving drunk. Take their keys. Carry a phone or change for a pay phone so you can call for a ride or a cab. Again, your friend may get upset, but that risk is less severe than the risk of a drunk-driving tragedy.

Get Help

If you are concerned that a friend or family member has a habit of drinking and driving, consider letting them know how you feel. Every situation is different, and you have to decide for yourself if a confrontation is a good idea. If you do decide to talk to your friend or family member, do it when he or she is sober. Be careful not to be accusatory; instead, let them know how worried you are about their safety. Repeated drunk driving can be a sign of a serious alcohol addiction. If you feel that your friend or loved one has an alcohol problem, consider seeking professional help. You might start with online resources, such as the Web site for the Hazelden Treatment Center (http://hazelden.optimaster.com). This site offers information and advice for people who have alcohol problems as well as those worried about friends and family members who suffer from substance abuse.

Take Action

Although drunk driving is a personal issue, it is also a social issue. If you are interested in attempting to make an impact on society by helping to save lives in an anti–drunk driving effort, there are various actions you can take. Consider joining a grassroots movement such as Mothers Against Drunk Driving (MADD) or Students Against Destructive Decisions (SADD). MADD offers advice on how to urge members of Congress to enact laws designed to stop drunk driving, fight underage drinking, and support victims of drunk-driving accidents. You can also volunteer with your local MADD chapter to provide direct assistance to victims of drunk-driving crashes, participate in public education efforts, and be a speaker at schools, civic groups, and other organizations.

SADD was originally formed as Students Against Drunk Driving, with a mission to help young people to not drink and drive. While the organization has expanded to address other goals, such as teenage pregnancy and violence, it is still committed to preventing drunk driving among youths. If you would like to get involved, join your local SADD chapter. If there is no SADD chapter at your school, church, or community center, consider forming one. The organization's Web site (www.SADD.org) can provide you with all the information you need in order to locate or form a new chapter. Some activities that SADD members undertake include campaigns to increase awareness of drunk driving, especially during high-risk periods such as homecoming and prom seasons.

Taking action is one way to address the problem of drunk driving. It is also important to know the law and to be prepared in case you find yourself in a risky situation. Never put yourself in danger by getting into a car when you or the driver have been drinking. Try your best to prevent others from driving drunk by educating them, taking their car keys, phoning for an alternative means of transportation, and talking to them about your concerns about their safety. The consequences are too drastic to simply go along with the crowd and get into a vehicle driven by someone whose skills have been impaired by alcohol.

American Beverage Institute (ABI)

1755 Pennsylvania Ave. NW, Suite 12000, Washington, DC 20006
(800) 843-8877
e-mail: abi@abionline.org
Web site: www.abionline.org

ABI is a restaurant trade association dedicated to promoting the responsible consumption of alcohol. ABI also sponsors studies by university researchers and traffic safety experts on the prevention of drunk driving and responsible consumption. The organization publishes the *ABI Newsletter* along with numerous reports on responsible drinking, the use of roadblocks, and the impact of .08 blood alcohol concentration (BAC) limits.

American Beverage Licensees (ABL)

5101 River Rd., Suite 108, Bethesda, MD 20816-1560
(301) 656-1494
Web site: www.ablusa.org

ABL is the nation's largest trade association dedicated to representing the interests of U.S. beer, wine, and spirits retailers. ABL represents nearly twenty thousand bars, restaurants, taverns, and liquor stores. ABL has members in 348 of the 435 congressional districts across the nation. The ABL Web site features research and information about responsible drinking.

Boaters Against Drunk Driving (BADD)

344 Clayton Ave., Battle Creek, MI 49017-5218
(269) 963-7068
e-mail: safeboating@badd.org
Web site: www.badd.org

BADD is dedicated to promoting safe, sober, and responsible boating throughout the United States and Canada. Through its Judicial

Watch, the organization monitors cases of individuals charged with boating under the influence of alcohol (BUI); BADD publishes the progress of these cases to demonstrate to the boating community and the general public that state boating officials, legislators, prosecutors, and courts all consider BUIs a very serious crime. BADD's Web site includes statistics, charts, and articles concerning the dangers of boating under the influence of alcohol.

Center for Substance Abuse Prevention (CSAP)
National Clearinghouse for Alcohol and Drug Prevention
PO Box 2345, Rockville, MD 20847-2345
(800) 729-6686
e-mail: info@health.org
Web site: www.health.org

The Center for Substance Abuse Prevention is the sole federal organization with responsibility for improving accessibility and quality of substance abuse prevention services. The center provides national leadership in the development of policies, programs, and services to prevent illegal drug use and underage alcohol and tobacco use. CSAP's Web site features information and research about alcohol and drug-addiction treatment and prevention.

Century Council
1310 G St. NW, Suite 600, Washington, DC 20005
(202) 637-0077
e-mail: kimballl@centurycouncil.org
Web site: www.centurycouncil.org

Funded by America's leading distillers, the Century Council is a not-for-profit national organization committed to fighting underage drinking and reducing alcohol-related crashes. The council promotes legislative efforts to pass tough drunk driving laws and works with the alcohol industry to help servers and sellers prevent drunk driving. The Century Council publishes information on stopping hardcore drunk drivers, educational information on blood alcohol concentration limits, and other topics related to drunk driving.

Entertainment Industries Council (EIC)
1760 Reston Pkwy., Suite 415, Reston, VA 20190-3303
(703) 481-1414
e-mail: eiceast@eiconline.org
Web site: www.eiconline.org

The Entertainment Industries Council is a nonprofit organization that works to educate the entertainment industry and audiences about major public health and social issues. Its members strive to effect social change by providing educational materials, research, and training to the entertainment industry. The EIC publishes several fact sheets concerning alcohol abuse and alcohol-impaired driving.

Mothers Against Drunk Driving (MADD)
511 John Carpenter Fwy., Suite 700, Irving, TX 75062
(800) GET-MADD
e-mail: info@madd.org
Web site: www.madd.org

MADD is a national grassroots organization whose mission is to stop drunk driving, support the victims of this violent crime, and prevent underage drinking. MADD has approximately six hundred chapters nationwide plus affiliates in Canada, Guam, Japan, Puerto Rico, and Sweden. MADD publicizes *Driven* magazine and numerous pamphlets and brochures. MADD also sponsors various programs for students, law enforcement officers, and other individuals with an interest in keeping America's roads safe.

National Commission Against Drunk Driving (NCADD)
8403 Colesville Rd., Suite 370, Silver Spring, MD 20910
(240) 247-6004
e-mail: info@ncadd.com
Web site: www.ncadd.com

The National Commission Against Drunk Driving is the successor to the Presidential Commission on Drunk Driving appointed by President Ronald Reagan in 1982 to develop the first report on this national problem. The mission of NCADD is to continue the efforts of the presidential commission to reduce impaired driving and its tragic consequences by uniting a broad-based coalition of public- and private-sector organizations and other concerned individuals who share this common purpose. The commission works closely with federal, state, and local officials as well as private-sector groups to develop strategies and programs to reduce the incidences of drunk driving.

National Highway Traffic Safety Administration (NHTSA)
400 Seventh St. SW, Washington, DC 20590
(888) 327-4236
Web site: www.nhtsa.gov

The NHTSA is committed to saving lives, preventing injuries, and reducing traffic-related health care and economic costs resulting from impaired driving. The NHTSA allocates funds for states to demonstrate the effectiveness of visible enforcement initiatives against drunk driving. The NHTSA conducts research and publishes reports and other materials to help educate the public, law enforcement professionals, and other individuals who play important roles in reducing the number of drunk drivers on the roads.

National Youth Rights Association (NYRA)
6930 Carroll Ave., Suite 610, Takoma Park, MD 20912
(301) 738-6769
e-mail: info@youthrights.org
Web site: www.youthrights.org

The National Youth Rights Association believes American youth alcohol policy should recognize the inevitability of alcohol consumption among youth and seek to reduce the harm of that alcohol use rather than unrealistically trying to keep young people from drinking at all. The NYRA publishes information and facts supporting a lower legal drinking age and studies on drunk driving.

Students Against Destructive Decisions (SADD)
255 Main St., Marlborough, MA 01752
(877) SADD-INC

e-mail: info@SADD.org
Web site: www.sadd.org

Formerly called Students Against Drunk Driving, SADD is a school-based organization dedicated to addressing the issues of underage drinking, impaired driving, drug use, and other destructive decisions that harm young people. SADD seeks to provide students with prevention and intervention tools that build the confidence needed to make healthy choices and behavioral changes. These tools include campaigns in honor of students killed in drunk driving accidents, impact scenarios, candlelight vigils, and student surveys on teens' attitudes and concerns about drinking and driving. SADD also holds conferences and publishes an annual newsletter.

Traffic Injury Research Foundation (TIRF)
171 Nepean St., Suite 200, Ottawa, ON K2P 0B4 Canada
(877) 238-5253
e-mail: deanm@trafficinjuryresearch.com
Web site: www.trafficinjuryresearch.com

The Traffic Injury Research Foundation is a national, independent road safety institute. Its mission is to reduce traffic-related deaths and injuries. Since its inception in 1964, TIRF has become internationally recognized for its accomplishments in a wide range of subject areas related to identifying the causes of road crashes and developing programs and policies to address them effectively.

BIBLIOGRAPHY

Books

Aaseng, Nathan, *Teens and Drunk Driving*. San Diego: Lucent Books, 2000.

Ammerman, Robert T., *Prevention and Societal Impact of Drug and Alcohol Abuse*. Mahwah, NJ: Lawrence Erlbaum Associates, 1999.

Bjorklund, Dennis A., *Drunk Driving Defense: How to Beat the Rap*. Iowa City: Praetorian, 1998.

Robert L. Dupont, *The Selfish Brain: Learning from Addiction*. Washington, DC: American Psychiatric Press, 1997.

Heather, Nick, and Tim Stockwell, *The Essential Handbook of Treatment and Prevention of Alcohol Problems*. Hoboken, NJ: Wiley, 2004.

Hempelman, Kathleen A., *Teen Legal Rights*. Westport, CT: Greenwood Press, 2000.

Knox, Jean McBee, *Drinking, Driving, and Drugs*. New York: Chelsea House, 1998.

Maruschak, Laura M., *DWI Offenders Under Correctional Supervision*. Washington, DC: U.S. Department of Justice, 1999.

McGowan, Richard, *Government Regulation of the Alcohol Industry: The Search for Revenue and the Common Good*. Westport, CT: Quorum Books, 1997.

Sloan, Frank A., ed., *Drinkers, Drivers, and Bartenders: Balancing Private and Public Accountability*. Chicago: University of Chicago Press, 2000.

Taylor, Lawrence, *Drunk Driving Defense*. Aspen, CO: Aspen, 2000.

Periodicals

Adlaf, Edward, et al., "Predictors of Completion Status in a Remedial Program for Male Convicted Drinking Drivers," *Journal of Studies on Alcohol*, May 2005.

Barakat, Matthew, "Judge Declares VA Drunk-Driving Laws Unconstitutional," *Chicago Daily Law Bulletin*, August 12, 2005.

Barone, Patrick T., and Jeffery S. Crampton, "Blood Alcohol Testing: Understanding Quantitative Blood Alcohol Testing in Drunk Driving Cases," *Michigan Bar Journal*, August 2003.

Bates, Betsy, "U.S. Women Are Closing Gap in Risky Drinking, Driving," *Family Practice News*, October 15, 2005.

Becker, Anne, "Ad Council Switches Slogans: Drunk-Driving Campaign Aims for Fresh Approach," *Broadcasting & Cable*, October 31, 2005.

Bergman, Hans, Beata Hubicka, and Hans Laurell, "Alcohol Problems and Blood Alcohol Concentration Among Swedish Drivers Suspected of Driving Under the Influence," *Contemporary Drug Problems*, Fall 2005.

Bingham, C. Raymond, and Jean T. Shope, "Drinking-Driving as a Component of Problem Driving and Problem Behavior in Young Adults," *Journal of Studies on Alcohol*, January 2002.

Carpenter, Christopher, "How Do Zero Tolerance Drunk Driving Laws Work?" *Journal of Health Economics*, January 2004.

Everson, Kirsten, "Drugged Driving," *Canadian Medical Association Journal*, January 3, 2006.

Flint, Joe, "In Face of Widening Backlash, NBC Gives Up Plan to Run Liquor Ads," *Wall Street Journal Western Edition*, March 21, 2002.

Foderaro, Lisa W., "Program Battles Drinking Long Before Drinking Age," *New York Times*, March 25, 2004.

Fulkerson, Andrew, "Blow and Go: The Breath-Analyzed Ignition Interlock Device as a Technological Response to DWI," *American Journal of Drug and Alcohol Abuse*, January 2003.

Marks, Paul, "Taking on the Drugged and Drunk Drivers: Roadside Devices to Test People's Motor Skills and Detect Drugs Might Help Police Make Traveling Safer," *New Scientist*, December 3, 2005.

Mejeur, Jeanne, "Still Driving Drunk: Strict Drunk Driving Laws Don't Do Much Good Unless They Are Vigorously Enforced," *State Legislatures*, December 2003.

Mothers Against Drunk Driving "MADD Says Youth Buying Alcohol," *Modern Brewery Age*, July 25, 2005.

Sarkar, Sheila, and Marie Andreas, "Acceptance of and Engagement in Risky Driving Behaviors by Teenagers," *Adolescence*, Winter 2004.

USA Today Magazine, "Hardcore Drinkers Are a National Plague," November 2005.

Yanovitzky, Itzhak, "Effect of News Coverage on the Prevalence of Drunk-Driving Behavior: Evidence from a Longitudinal Study," *Journal of Studies on Alcohol*, May 2002.

Web Sites

Alcohol Awareness Research Library (www.alcoholstats.com). This site provides information about drunk driving, underage drinking, alcohol abuse, and responsible alcohol consumption. It also includes statistics on the rate of drunk driving and number of fatalities caused by drunk driving for each state.

Drunk Driving Education and Information (www.dui.com/). A comprehensive site that contains articles and research about many aspects of drunk driving, including recent court decisions about driving under the influence, state laws, and adolescent drunk driving.

PICTURE CREDITS

ABOUT THE EDITOR

Christine Van Tuyl graduated magna cum laude from the University of California, San Diego, with a degree in communications. She has worked as a writer for a television news station in San Diego and as a publicist for several local organizations. Currently, she works as a freelance writer, editing books on social issues and current events, as well as writing restaurant and nightlife reviews for an entertainment Web site.